"IF THESE WALLS COULD TALK..."

An Easy Guide to Tracking Your House's Genealogy

by

Maurcia DeLean Houck

PICTON PRESS
ROCKPORT, MAINE

All photographs were taken by the author, unless otherwise noted and all illustrations were drawn by Robert Montgomery.

First Printing July 1999

This book is available from:

Picton Press
PO Box 250
Rockport, ME 04856-0250

Visa/MasterCard orders:
1-207-236-6565
FAX orders: 1-207-236-6713
www.pictonpress.com

Manufactured in the United States of America
Printed on 60# acid-free paper

∞

TABLE OF CONTENTS

ACKNOWLEDGMENTS

No book is written by a single person. It takes encouragement and guidance from many voices to get an author through the trials of writing a book. I am no exception.

While I clearly understand that there were far too many people involved in making this book a reality to list them all, I also acknowledge that there were a handful of individuals who deserve special recognition for the integral part they played in bringing *If These Walls Could Talk* to its reader.

First and foremost I'd like to give a great big hug of thanks to my publisher, Lew Rohrbach, my editor, Candy McMahan Perry, as well as the staff at Picton Press. Many other publishers showed an interest in this project, but you were the only one willing to take the risk on this relatively unknown writer. You'll never know how much I appreciate the faith you placed in me through this project.

To Mary and Jack Washington, two people whose love for historic houses must be contagious! If it weren't for your excitement for house genealogy, I may never have "caught the bug."

To The Old York Road Historical Society in Jenkintown, Pa. Thanks so much for all your help in finding just the right pictures for this book.

To Robert Montgomery, a very talented illustrator and friend. Thanks for adding that extra special touch.

To my friends and family. Without your encouragement and love, I would have given up years ago.

And to my husband, Dave, who's lived through temper tantrums, deadlines, and piles & piles of research books and papers to get this book done. I love you.

Finally, to my daughter Kendra, who has taught me the importance of preserving our past, so that we may more fully appreciate our future.

PREFACE

When my friends Mary and Jack bought their house, they knew it was old. And needed repairs — lots and lots of repairs. What they didn't learn until years later, was that their home wasn't just another *old house.* It's an historic landmark that dates back to the early 1600s.

How did they unravel the mystery? Their house told them! Oh, not in so many words, but the clues were there: dates inscribed on attic beams, antique bottles unearthed in the backyard, a capped well near the back door, and their most amazing discovery to date — an original beehive oven hidden behind a plaster living room wall.

Using these few clues, Mary and Jack set off on a quest to unravel their house's long and intricate past ... and so can you. Every house has a history. Setting out to learn about that history can be fascinating. Your home doesn't have to be as old as Mary and Jack's to sport intriguing tales of the people who once inhabited its rooms, or even the neighborhood where it's located. My own home is less than 50 years old, yet I've uncovered a few interesting tidbits regarding the plot of land where it now stands.

If you're interested enough in your house's story to read this book, I assume you're interested enough to embark on a journey full of twists and turns, not to mention a few surprises. Like my friends, some of you reading *If These Walls Could Talk* may walk away from the search having unearthed enough information to boost your property value. Others will have to settle for learning ordinary facts about ordinary people who lived ordinary lives within the same rooms your family now occupies. Either way, my hope is that each of you reading this book will find a deeper understanding for the place you call home.

Before you begin, let me add one small warning. A genealogical search of any kind requires a great deal of interest and patience, not to mention persistence. This guide is not meant to make the search simple. *If These Walls Could Talk* does promise to walk hand-in-hand with you through each and every step of your own historic trail.

Together, we'll head off on a paper chase scouring the basement rooms of your local courthouse, state archives, historical society and newspaper morgue, to find the documentation you'll need to trace your house's complete history.

Next, we'll check the house itself for structural and construction clues in order to properly date it.

Finally, I'll explain how to give your home historic status through local, state and federal registers.

The journey ahead may be long, and it may be difficult. But who knows, like Mary and Jack, you too may find yourself — and your house — becoming a part of history.

Good luck and Happy Tracking!

SECTION I :

THE PAPER CHASE

CHAPTER ONE:
Your First Stop: The Courthouse

You're about to embark on a wonderful adventure. In the weeks to come you'll blaze your own personal trail of history. One that uncovers the secrets of your house. Are you ready? Then, let's get started.

Your first stop is the courthouse. It's a gold mine of information containing records on every property within the district. Plan on spending several days — or even weeks — scouring its countless records and indexes. In this one building alone, you'll discover hundreds of facts about your home, including who else has owned it, what they paid for it, what it looked like decades ago, what (if any) structural changes have taken place through the years, and more.

The best place to begin is at the Recorder of Deeds Office. In some states this department is called the Register Conveyer, Circuit Clerk, County Recorder, or the County Auditor.

I will assume that you already have the most recent deed filed on your property. You should have received an updated copy shortly after you bought your house. Make several copies of it. It's here that your search begins.

The deed may be the single most important document in unlocking a house's past.

In it you'll find references to previous deeds, the books where they are recorded, and even the page number where the entry can be found. This nugget of information will start you on the long trek to tracing the chain of title to your property. But first, let's talk a little about deeds.

Grantor — the individual(s) selling the property
Grantee — the individual(s) buying the property

What are deeds? Simply put, they are a record of land ownership. An invaluable resource for the researcher, deeds offer important clues to the names of the grantors (sellers), grantees (buyers), sale prices, dates of transfer and descriptions of properties.

Although deeds from individual states — and even time periods — may look different, they all contain about the same information.

There are two basic deed styles to be aware of: the indenture deed and the deed poll. They may look a lot alike (except for the language featured), but there is one main difference: the location of the transfer date.

The date of transfer is located at the bottom of a deed poll instead of the beginning, like it is in an indenture deed. This is important to remember, otherwise you may find yourself cross-eyed and frustrated because you can't find the date of record.

Like any legal document, deeds can be difficult to read, thanks to their complicated legal rambling.

Despite their differences, however, you can count on many deeds following this simple format, or one somewhat similar to it: First, you'll notice a recitation of events leading up to the transfer such as a sale or death. Next, there'll be a list of names (the grantors, grantees and witnesses). A detailed description of the property follows, with the sale price next, and finally ending with information on how the grantor obtained the property and the necessary signatures.

Deed — **formal contract indicating the legal transfer of property**

Other things to look for are:

deed book numbers and page references

transfer and recording dates

acreage

outer building listings (taverns, barns ,etc).

In short, your job is to spot anything out of the ordinary.

Locating the oldest deeds to a property isn't an easy task. It takes more than walking into the Recorder's Office and asking to see all of their deeds. Chances are, newer deeds recorded within the last 25-50 years are available on microfilm or computers. But it'll be up to you to search for older versions. Sometimes this will mean scouring dozens of indexes in a makeshift library. Or it may entail spending hours sifting through record boxes in a musty basement.

How then, do you find the deeds you're looking for? Most are categorized using deed indexes. Every index is arranged differently, depending on whatever bookkeeping system the Recorder used at the time. Most, however, are alphabetized by either the first letter of the surname, the first letter of the given name, or chronologically. Don't be surprised to discover that many records are stored using various methods, depending on the point in history in which the documents were recorded.

Once you find the deeds you're looking for, the next step is figuring out how to read them. That may sound easy enough. It isn't always. Deeds have the tendency to ramble. What's worse, the older the deed, the older the language. Until the researcher becomes familiar with these unknown terms, this antiquated terminology can put a quick halt to the most ardent search.

Abbreviations present problems too. Many Recorders developed their own form of shorthand, which can oftentimes be nearly impossible to decipher. For a listing of common abbreviations and historic usages see the accompanying the end of this chapter.

Understanding property descriptions can also be difficult. Most won't make much sense at first, but you'll soon get the knack for it and be able to read even the toughest descriptions.

For instance, many deeds describe property lines in view of things that were once (but are no longer), located on the property site, such as stones, trees, and fences.

A description might read something like this: *starts at the large oak on the north side and runs south along the stone wall, ending at the boulder on the far southwest corner.* How in the world are you expected to figure out where the original property lines begins and ends? We'll discuss other sources that can help you, later in this chapter.

Another obstacle many researchers encounter is deciphering measuring devices. The metes and bounds (measures and boundaries) of a deed are often specified using points of reference, (as mentioned above), compass directions, and distances in regards to neighboring landowners using perches in conjunction with simple geometric principles.

Points of reference can be trees, stones and even buildings.

Compass directions are critical components of the description. To determine the compass direction you must remember that a circle is composed of 360 degrees. The compass is divided into four 90 degree quadrants (north, south, east and west). In course designations, the first compass direction given is the starting point for calculating the course, with a number of degrees toward the next direction given. South twenty degrees east means you start at the direction south, and proceed twenty degrees east. This is the direction you'll measure toward, from your point of reference.

Perch — **a unit of measure equaling 5.5 yards**

Compass directions usually start at north or south and proceed in degrees running east and west.

Distances create a whole new set of problems. Surveyors measure in the form of perches. A perch measures 16.5 feet or 5.5 yards. When determining the area of a plot, the perch reference means square perch. For example an acre would equal 160 square perches.

Some other terms you'll need to know:

A *Rod*, which is the same as a perch

A *Pole* is also the same as a perch

A *Chain* equals 4 perches or 66 feet or 22 yards

A *Link* measures 7.92 inches.

One hundred *links* make up one *Chain*

An *Acre* is 43,560 square feet

A *Rood* is a 1/4 acre or 40 square perches

Tracing a deed may sound easy enough, but dead ends — or deeds that don't refer to other deeds — do occur. Sometimes it's because no deeds were ever filed prior to a specific date. Or the property changes hands some other way as is the case when a property changes hands via an inheritance. When this happens, you'll need to continue tracing your house's history using other types of courthouse records.

But first, double-check the grantor/grantee indexes to see if the deed was filed there instead. When that strategy fails, it's time to move from the Recorder of Deeds to a new office.

- MORTGAGES & SHERIFF DEEDS -

Mortgages are very common nowadays. Very few people can afford a home without one. That wasn't always the case. In the past, many houses were bought and sold on a cash basis.

That said, mortgages were sometimes taken on a property — and filed with a property's deed — when the owner came upon hard times and needed to borrow against his property.

When a loan, such as a mortgage, is paid in full, the deed book records the transaction with the clause "Provided Always," or "Satisfied." Paid mortgages don't offer much information about a given property other than the fact that it was once used to secure a loan.

When a mortgage-holder fails to pay off a mortgage agreement, the property can be forfeited and sold to pay the bad debt, leaving an indispensable paper trail for the house genealogist to follow.

Before a property is auctioned off to satisfy a debt, the mortgage holder must first sue the mortgagee for the amount of the outstanding debt. A writ *fieri facias* (fi.fa) is usually then issued by the court. This authorizes the sheriff to levy goods on the debtor's personal property. If the goods received are insufficient to pay off the debt, a writ of *venditioni exponas* (vend.ex) then allows the sheriff to seize the property for public sale.

A sheriff's deed, also known as a deed poll, offers many wonderful clues to a house's history. It not only recites the long legal proceedings required to seize the property, it also names the plaintiff, lists the date each writ was issued, the date of the auction, and more.

The house genealogist can use all of this information to locate newspaper advertisements featuring the sale. When found, these can offer greater insight regarding what the house looked like since they often describe the property down to the minutest detail — even the furniture which graced its rooms.

Grantor	GEORGE D. WIDNER, et ux, et al
Grantee	PETER A. B. WIDENER
Date of Transfer	November 12, 1896
Recorded Montgomery County Deed Book	417 Page 216
Transcribed by E. M.	Checked by J. ?. ?. Date 9/1/38

Description of Property

ALL THAT CERTAIN LOT OR PIECE OF GROUND

One Thereof: Beginning at a corner the intersection
of the middle line of Chelten Ave. and ### Serpentine/and ^{Lane}
being also a corner of ground now or lateof said Thomas
Mellor; thence along the middle line of Serpentine, the 7
following courses and distances, viz: N. 37 deg. 38' East
192.06'; N. 65 deg. 42' East 205.26', N. 88 deg. 28' East
192.72', the last three courses by ground now or late of
Thomas Mellor; thence S. 79 deg. 46' East by ground now or
late of Fib. Birck, 271.92' thence S. 74 deg. 29' East 429.01'
S. 61 deg. 40' East 206.58', S. 84 deg. 4' East 217.14', the
last three courses being by ground now or late of Jay Cook;
thence leaving the Serpentine/and still by land now or late ^{Lane}
of the said Jay Cook, S. 41 deg. West 913.4' to a corner in
the middle line of Chelten Ave., now Ashbourne Rd., being
also a corner of John W. Thomas, thence along the middle line
of said Chelten Ave., now Ashbourne Rd. by land now or late of
the said John W. Thomas, N. 58 deg. 40' West 466.29' to a stone
in the middle line of said Chelten Ave. being also a corner of
the tract of land next hereinafter described; thence by the sam
and still along the middle line of said Chelten Ave. now

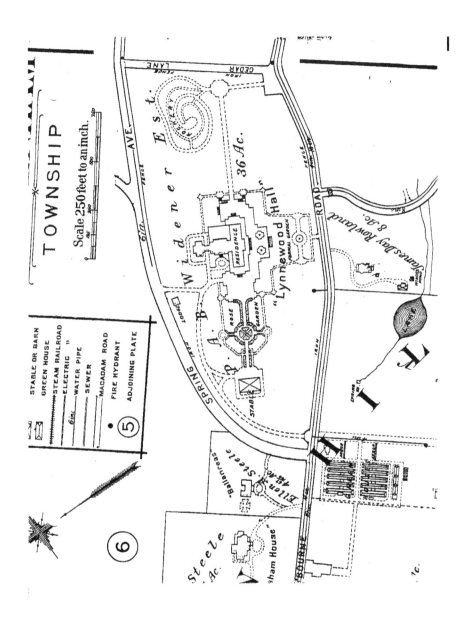

Road maps prove that your house existed during a specific period in your town's history

These records are most often found right alongside regular deeds in the county deed books. Some may also be filed with Appearance Dockets of the Court of Common Pleas records.

- WILLS & ORPHAN COURT RECORDS -

When someone dies, the probate court appoints an executor to inventory the deceased person's estate and estimate its value. Settlement records often give a complete picture of the home, farm or business property as well as personal items. Income and expense records may also be included, shedding some light on the previous owner's financial status.

Executor — a person appointed to execute a will

Wills, too, sometimes list furnishings and valuables room-by-room, giving the home researcher an excellent idea of what the interior of the house looked like during a specific era.

Outside property references such as a blacksmith's shed or barn can also yield important clues by showing the day-to-day workings on the property. While researching a local estate for my neighborhood newspaper several years ago, I learned that the property was its own self-contained community, complete with a butcher's shed, blacksmith's shop, etc. Had I failed to take notice of the numerous outbuildings and what they were used for, I would have missed an important link of history regarding that particular property.

Wills are generally filed alphabetically. If no settlement records or wills can be found, orphans' court records may have what you're looking for. In the case of more than one heir (especially minors), where no will can be found, the orphans' court is the entity which distributes property among the heirs by either selling it or dividing the property into sections. Such a draft of division can be used to locate a single plot within the larger tract of land prior to any subdivision.

Probate Court — a court which handles the administration of wills

-PLAT MAPS -

Most of today's neighborhoods were once large tracts of land belonging to one person or family. Over the last one hundred years or so, these large tracts in most areas (both urban and rural), have been divided into the small lots most of us now own.

Plat maps are plans of an area that show the boundaries of individual properties. They can be used to trace these changes of ownership for both your own property, and that of your neighbors, by locating the smaller plots that have been subdivided again and again from older farms and estates.

Measurements registered on plat maps before the 20th century are often referred to in units known as Links (7.92") and chains (100 links). After 1900 these surveys often sported today's common measurements of a standard foot (12").

-TAX RECORDS -

No one who owns land can get away without paying property taxes. Luckily for the researcher, these records are all in the public domain.

Property taxes are levied on the basis of an assessed value of both the land and the buildings that sit on it. Changes in these levied taxes may indicate improvements to a property. For instance, an assessed value that jumps sharply from one tax year to the next is a good indicator that a large addition or improvement was completed on the house. Always double check these suspicions with other tax records to rule out an across the board rise in assessed values.

Public Domain— an unprotected copyright available for all citizens to review.

-BUILDING PERMITS -

If your research has left you wondering about a major renovation project on the property, double check that assumption with local building permit records. Although common in urban areas, these may not be as readily available in rural ones where residents may not have been required to file for such permits.

**Building Permit —
official permission to
complete a building**

When available, building permit records can lead you on a wonderful discovery about the changes your house has undergone over the years. Many not only show the dates of renovations, estimated costs, and building dimensions, but may even include detailed architectural designs. They can also be used to figure out when repairs and remodeling such as the installation of indoor plumbing and electricity were installed in an historic home.

- ROAD RECORDS -

A major responsibility of any municipality is to lay out public roads. Chances are the roads in your community began as mere paths or cart ways, suitable for wagons. Later, some may have become turnpikes and toll roads operated by the state. Today, some roads are maintained by your local township, others by the state or federal government.

The procedures for laying out roads (both now and in the past), result in a complex series of records. The one found most useful by the house genealogist is the surveyors' drafts of proposed roads. They were known to show where houses sat along a proposed thoroughfare during the year the roadway was proposed.

- MECHANICS LIENS -

Since the early 1800s, tradesmen and builders have been able to legally collect unpaid balances for their work by instituting a mechanics lien on a property. Sometimes, these liens (which are filed with a house's deed), contain details about the work that was done on the house and even the materials used on the remodeling projects.

Having now completed the part of your search that takes place in the local courthouse, it's time to move onto the State Archives. Used in conjunction with the records you've already compiled, they too, will help fill in some of the gaps about your house's story, especially those left open by unavailable or incomplete local records.

WHERE TO FIND LOCAL RECORDS:

There are several places you can turn to get information on the history of your house. Among them are:

City Hall:
Your local municipalities office is a good place to locate building permits, electrical and plumbing inspection records, tax plats, and various maps of the township or borough.

County Records Office:
Here you'll find deeds, wills, tax records mortgages and liens.

Historical Societies:
Historical Societies are chock full of interesting information about the region, which may include specific information on your property. Among the many finds hidden away in local historical society archives are: personal diaries; architectural designs; various maps; old advertisements; local histories; photographs; personal inventories; local directories; etc.

Newspaper Morgues:
The local newspaper archives often referred to as the "morgue" offer a unique peek into the past. Old newspaper clippings yield a myriad of information on ownerships, previous fires, floods and other natural disasters which may have affected the property; debates and controversies surrounding the property; sheriff sale notices and real estate advertisements, among others.

Probate Office:
Wills, inventories and orphan's court records are found in this office.

COMMON ABBREVIATIONS

Your research will undoubtedly uncover many types of abbreviations, especially within early American documents. Although many writers and recorders developed their own personal forms of abbreviations, these are a few of the most commonly used:

accord	— according	*inventory*	— invent, inv
administration	— admin, admon	*namely*	— viz
		paid	— p
aforesaid	— afors, afsd	*received*	— rec, recv
and	— &	*receipt*	— rec
deceased	— dec	*record*	— rec
executor	— exec., ex	*register*	— reg, regist
improvement	— improv	*the*	— ye

SPECIAL KINDS OF DEEDS

Deed of Assignment
authorizes the sale of a property to satisfy all outstanding debts held by the owner.

Deed of Gift
a deed like any other deed, except that it conveys the property as a gift from the grantor to the grantee. To meet legal requirements, most transfers state a minimum $1 purchase price.

Deed of Release
returns the property title back to the grantee following a mortgage payoff.

Claim Deed
a release of all property claims to the grantee. Most commonly used to correct errors made by a surveyor in establishing the property's boundaries.

Release
a deed used to forfeit rights to a property, as in the case of one business or marriage partner releasing his/her property rights to the other partner.

Trust Deed
conveys land to a trustee for a certain purpose (ie: for use as a school, church, etc.) May also be held in trust for a person, usually a minor child.

CHAPTER TWO:
State Findings

If local records left a hole in your research, try the state archives. They may be able to help you fill in some of the gaps.

Most states hold a variety of local, state and federal records in their archives. Oftentimes, older city records are even shipped to the state archives for safe keeping when the local municipality runs out of storage space.

Where can you find state records? Like local governments, each state compiles its records according to its own individual storage system. Some have state-run libraries or archives, while others hand their records over to state historical societies for indexing. Most, however, are located in offices within or near the capitol. To find out what types of records your state archives have, call or write for a pamphlet describing their collection and a directory of other repositories.

Repository — a place housing records and documents of historic significance

Archives — a place housing governmental and historic records

What can you expect to find there? Some of the most common documents stored in the state archives are:

- LAND GRANTS/PATENTS -

The earliest kind of land record is a grant of land which deeds sections of land to its very first owner. Readers living in the midwest or western sections of the country will find these records through the national government (see CHAPTER THREE). Easterner's residing in the original colonies, however, will find these records most usually at their state archives.

The first step to obtaining a copy of an original Land Grant is locating the appropriate Land Grant Index. Here you'll find the name of the first grantee, acreage amount and grant number. With this number, you'll be able to request a copy of the original grant and its accompanying survey.

One disadvantage to tracing your property back to its original land grant owner is the fact that the grant itself may not specify any one piece of land. In some cases, the grants were issued before the new owner ever left his homeland. Therefore, the property purchased was written in acreage amounts, not set plots. This enabled the grantee to choose the final location of his property when he got to the colonies. Once he'd chosen his plot, the grantee was issued a land warrant, followed by an official survey which established the property's formal boundaries. Lastly, a final land patent or deed was issued.

Land Grant— a grant of land from the government

When tracing land grants and patents, it is important for you to remember that land was rarely purchased or sold in individual lots, as is common in the 20th century. Until recent years, most grantees purchased very large tracts of land that were later subdivided again and again, resulting in today's individual house lots. This may make it very difficult to locate your specific property on a land grant. They are useful, however, in determining the size of an original tract of land and its ownership.

-TERRITORIAL PAPERS -

Territorial Papers were the only form of official record-keeping before a territory received its official statehood. These records include a variety of documents dealing with a variety of issues including land distribution, property transfers, militia muster rolls, voter lists, jury lists, road requests, and more.

Some territorial records are housed by their respective state, while others have been shipped to their regional office of the National Archives. If your state no longer holds possession of these records, try finding them in the *Territorial Papers of the United States,* a comprehensive listing of territorial records compiled and published by the Government Printing Office for the State Department and the National Archives. Most large public, research and university libraries either own a copy, or have access to one through interlibrary loan.

Interlibrary Loan — **a system coordinating the loan of reference materials from one library to another**

- ROAD RECORDS -

Roads connect our communities and states to one another. Some are under the auspices of local government, state transportation department, or the federal government.

Turnpikes and toll roads are generally built and maintained by the state government, making their records available at the state archive level.

Before any road is built, often it is first requested by the area residents, who submit a formal petition outlining their reasons for asking for a roadway. Once a petition is accepted, surveyors are sent to draft the proposed road. Old surveys often mention houses and buildings situated along the new byway.

These state roadway records are often kept using an "index to Roads," arranged by township or county. They are stored in either the department of transportation or the state archives.

- SURVEYOR'S RECORDS -

Land surveys are taken to determine the boundaries of a property. It is rare for a surveyor's notes and sketches to include information about the placement of houses on the property. These records do offer a unique glimpse of property divisions and boundary disputes that have occurred over the years.

Original surveys are stored with land grants. Later surveys are commonly found filed with other legal documents such as deeds, and orphans' court records. Some, less formal versions, may also turn up in collections of private papers and wills.

- CENSUS RECORDS -

State censuses, were sometimes taken in addition to the federal census (federal censuses are taken every ten years beginning in 1790). State censuses were completed for several reasons:

* to determine a territory's eligibility for statehood
* taxation purposes
*military service recruitments

House genealogists may not glean much help from state census records. Some states don't take them. Others gather only statistical information. There are a few, though, that show in-depth surveys on the property owners acquisitions (including their home), as well as family.

Census — a formal population count which may also include property evaluations.

Territory — a part of the United States not included within any state

- TAX LISTS -

Similar to local tax lists, state taxation documents record rates and personal property inventories back to colonial times. In some communities, local tax records may not be available. In such cases, copies are just one of the many types of documents filed at the state archives.

-INDEX OF ECONOMIC MATERIALS -

If you're looking for more in depth knowledge on a particular individual, town or institution's economy, the series title *Index of Economic Materials* is a good place to start. This is a great time saver since it amasses many different kinds of state documents within one easy-to-use set of indexes.

Compiled in the early part of the 20th century by the Carnegie Institute, the series offers comprehensive indexes to printed reports of departments and legislatures within California (1849-1904); Delaware (1789-1904); Illinois (1809-1904); Kentucky (1792-1904); Maine (1820-1904); Massachusetts (1789-1904); New Hampshire

(1789-1904); New Jersey (1789-1904); New York (1789-1904); Ohio (1787-1904); Pennsylvania (1790-1904); Rhode Island (1789-1904); and Vermont (1789-1904).

They contain all kinds of economic information on the states listed, which often include information on specific individuals, companies and towns. They are indexed chronologically under such topics as: agriculture, education, mining, climate, state roads, population, etc.

Even if you can't uncover any information regarding your specific home or its previous owners, the *Index of Economic Material* is an excellent resource for establishing the lifestyles and state of the economy of the community, and even unusual weather patterns during specific periods in history.

-AERIAL PHOTOGRAPHS -

Aerial photographs were taken for many reasons: to study the earth's surface for military purposes, land use and geographic changes and to document the addition of man-made structures such as dams.

Although not generally taken to document specific properties, many do record building increases in certain areas and neighborhoods. If you're lucky, you may be able to find your home on these photos and physically view any major changes.

- COURT RECORDS -

CIVIL: The only civil court record that has any real bearing to the history of a house is a proceeding known as Ejectment. When two parties found themselves arguing over ownership (often in the case over disputed boundary line, divorce, or in the case of squatters and tenants who refused to leave), they could apply for a writ of ejectment. This allowed the court to decide who rightfully held title to the property.

CRIMINAL: The prosecution of criminal violations against a house or property can take several forms: burglary, assault, murder. While any of these may offer an interesting twist to a house's overall history, the most enlightening criminal cases would revolve around arson, or the deliberate setting of fire with the intent to destroy the property.

Evidence of a major fire at any building is an important discovery. Add to that the drama of arson and you've just added a new chapter to your house's biography. These records may also help you properly date existing buildings. For instance, if you discover a house was burned to the ground in 1910, then you can assume the house you live in now was built sometime after that.

There is a major obstacle to using these types of records. In most cases, the documentation is listed under the defendant's (or the arsonists) name, and not the homeowner's. The owner may be listed in the docket as a witness.

Unless you've uncovered more information about the fire using other sources such as newspaper accounts or private diaries, your chances of ever stumbling across these records are slim.

- HISTORIC REGISTERS -

A building doesn't have to have been the home of a famous person or the site of an historically significant event to be placed on a historic register.

Many states have named historic districts simply as a way to acknowledge structural significance, age or the need for historic preservation in a given area. Oftentimes, these districts were established years ago with no further require-

Historic District — a neighborhood or town given special historic status

ments except for a proclamation filed with the town charter or state. Other states significantly mark these districts and establish set rules for their general upkeep and renovation.

A quick check with your local township office, city hall or state historical commission can tell you if your community sports such a district and whether or not your home is on it.

Houses may also be individually listed for historic status. Again, the rules and regulations for this type of register differ from state to state and municipality to municipality.

Discovering that your house has been listed on either a local, state or national register makes your job as a house genealogist a lot easier.

In order for a property to be listed on this type of register, a good deal of research must have already been completed and filed on it. These records will be available with the office in charge of historic registrations.

For more information on how you can register your property on an historic register see CHAPTER THIRTEEN.

- OTHER RECORDS -

In conjunction with the records already described, there are numerous other documents which find their way into state archives. They include cemetery records, personal collections, genealogical notes and collections of maps. All may be helpful in your search, depending on the types of information you've already gathered and exactly what you're looking for.

(Courtesy of the Old York Road Historical Society)
Ariel photographs like this 1950s one of Jenkintown, PA can give you a good idea of the history of a neighborhood.

WRITING FOR RECORDS

It's best to conduct your own research personally. After all, you're not always sure exactly what you're looking for. Sometimes, the best nuggets of information uncovered are the ones you never even thought of. This said, I realize it isn't always possible to spend long days searching through records, especially when those records are housed in state archives hundreds of miles away from home.

When writing for records is the only possible option, there are a few pointers you need to keep in mind:

* *BE BRIEF* — nothing turns off administrators and research assistants more than blabbering letters. Don't beat around the bush. If you know what you need, say so — briefly and succinctly. Include only pertinent information such as proper names, dates, addresses and documentation needed.

* *ASK SPECIFIC QUESTIONS:* Asking for "whatever you have on 100 Main Street, Anytown," isn't going to get you much. Such in-depth requests usually end up in either the trash bin or in someone's "later" file. Instead, ask for tax records for a specific date; a title search on a single property; or an historic photograph taken at a certain time.

* *BE POLITE.* Nobody likes to be taken for granted. This is especially true for office personnel willing to help you on your search. Always be kind, sincere and grateful in your correspondence.

* *SEND APPROPRIATE FEES.* There are often charges associated with mail order research. Depending on the depth of your query, you may be charged only minimal copy charges or you may be charged hefty research fees. Better check on the costs involved before making an official query, which could result in an official bill.

* *ENCLOSE PROPER SASE (self addressed stamped envelope).* This is not only a polite gesture, it also aids in a quicker return of your requested documents since they can be easily dropped into the envelope, sealed and mailed without someone taking the extra time to address an envelope and put it through the postage meter.

FINDING YOUR STATE'S RECORDS

For a comprehensive listing of your state's historic preservation offices, archives, research libraries and repositories, check your telephone book or call the state capitol.

For a state-by-state guide, turn to *The State Executive Directory,* distributed by Carroll Publishing Company. This handy reference lists most state offices, their corresponding personnel and numbers for direct telephone access.

USING INTERLIBRARY LOAN

No library can afford (or has the space) to stock every book or periodical you may need to complete your research project. That's where Interlibrary Loan comes in. It is a service library reference departments use to exchange or loan reference materials.

As a subscriber, the library has access to millions of books across the country, in both public and private libraries. Expect to pay a small fee for the service.

In some cases, you may find that the documents you seek are unavailable for loan through ILL. Once your home-librarian has located them, it may be possible to contact the other facilities' librarian personally to request a copy of the records or book pages needed.

Other options include downloading information via your library's computer system. Many libraries, especially private repositories, have used scanners to make fragile documents more accessible to researchers. These scanned images can easily be sent (via e-mail transmission) to your library's computer and printed out for use. Again, processing fees are common. You may also be asked to pay any long-distance phone charges since, depending on the size of the document you're requesting, the download time could be quite long.

CHAPTER THREE:
Ask Uncle Sam

The United States government is a goldmine of information with literally *millions* of records in its possession. Housed in the National Archives in Washington D.C., many date as far back as the Revolutionary War and the Continental Congress, and some even earlier.

The sheer volume of these federal documents make it impossible to list every book, report or record that can be used to research a house's history. This chapter will, however, highlight some of the records other house genealogists have found useful.

In most cases, it will not be necessary to search every type of record described in this chapter. Land was acquired by many different methods over the years, leaving behind many different types of documents recording transfers. Once you locate the information on a particular owner or period in history you're after, move on.

- LAND RECORDS -

People have been filing land records since the first colonists built their settlements. Originally housed in the General Land Office of the United States, these historic records have been moved to the National Archives with other important historic documents.

What can national land records tell you about your property? Land records give basic information such as: who settled the land, how they acquired it, and even the original purchase price. Personal information regarding the owners is also plentiful in many of these older documents. They can also give more interesting facts like whether *General Land Office* — a territory office handling all land transfers and disputes

or not a railroad, mining camp or even an Indian Reservation ever sat on the site.

Original land grants were issued in three steps: warrants, surveys and patents.

First, the grantee applied for a warrant. It was a government document authorizing the Surveyor General of the area to lay out boundaries for the purchase.

Once the Surveyor General received the warrant, he was free to go out to the site and survey it, recording its exact measurements with the land office.

That done, the purchaser could apply for and receive a patent, the final version of the deed, releasing the land to the grantee legally.

Although the steps to obtaining a land grant are the same, there have been several ways that land has been transferred from one entity to another throughout our country's long history. Each sports its own kind of record. Here are just a few:

CREDIT ENTRY FILES

From 1800 to 1820, anyone buying public land did so using a five-year payment plan subsidized by the federal government. This created a stream of paperwork that's very useful to today's researcher.. Credit Entry Certificates (called *Credit Prior Certificates* before 1820 and *Credit Under Certificates* after 1820), were issued on all completed transactions.

CASH ENTRY FILES

Beginning in 1820, the federal government stopped selling land on credit and turned instead to a cash-only system. These *cash entry certificates* were issued to all purchasers at the time of transfer.

MILITARY BOUNTY APPLICATIONS

To encourage enlistments and to reward military service, the government offered free land between the Revolutionary War and the early 1900's. Many veterans took advantage of this free land, leaving behind a paper trail on the properties they acquired.

HOMESTEAD FILES

In 1862 the United States government passed The Homestead Act, which gave people the right to claim land free of charge if they could prove that they had settled and improved it over a specific time span. These homestead entries are filed under two separate series — those that were completed and those that weren't.

Homestead — **tracts acquired from U.S. public lands by filing a record, living on and cultivating the land**

PRIVATE CLAIMS

The National Archives has private land claim records for 15 states: Illinois, Indiana, Michigan, Wisconsin, Alabama, Mississippi, Louisiana, Missouri, Arkansas, Iowa, Florida, Arizona, California, Colorado and New Mexico. Private claim records include surveyor's reports and plats; congressional reports and various maps, among other items.

MODERN DAY LAND ENTRIES

Abstract Book — **an index of land transfer summaries**
Tract Books — **an index of land tracts**

All land records from 1908 to 1973 are filed together using only the patent number. They are alphabetized by both the applicant's name and the land office.

When researching land records, keep in mind that those from the original states, plus Maine, Vermont, West Virginia, Kentucky, Tennessee, Texas and Hawaii, are not located in the National Archives, but in each state's capitol.

If you live in a western state you may be able to access original tract books, abstract books, land entry case files, survey plats and correspondence relating to each of these types of land entries at the National Archives.

To search the records of public land states and territories, you will need some basic information:

* applicant's name
* land description (township, range, section)
* name of land office
* type of transfer
* certificate number

Name indexes to land entries will give you this basic information. They are available for many states from 1800 to the 1900s.

- CENSUS RECORDS -

Taken every ten years since 1790 as a way to determine each state's correct representation in the House of Representatives, this type of population count offers more than numbers. Census schedules are chock full of tidbits relating to the individual properties and businesses listed, as well as their owners.

Before turning to these national archive records, keep in mind that not all census records are available to the general public. Federal Law requires that all census records be kept confidential for 72 years, making only those before the 1930 census currently open to the public.

When seeking specific information, it's best to skip the earliest census records. The very first ones that were taken offer fragmented information at best. Oftentimes, the only thing they even list is the name of the head of the household. Records taken after 1850 are more in depth. They include such things as the names, ages and places of birth of each household resident.

Census — a formal population count taken by the federal government every ten years

With so many census records, searching for just the right entry may seem a taunting task. The actual search shouldn't be as tough as it first appears. Schedules for individual states are indexed separately, with records alphabetized by county. They are available for loan or purchase on microfilm for easy retrieval.

Requests for census records must be submitted on specific forms. Have the name of the county, state, census year, page number (found in the index) and enumeration district number (for records between 1880-1920), when making all inquiries. You can obtain the appropriate forms by contacting any National Archives Regional Office. For the address and telephone number of the office nearest you, see the listing at the end of this chapter.

In conjunction with the basic census, these other supplemental census schedules may be helpful in your search:

THE MANUFACTURER'S CENSUS, taken from 1820-1832, was a special census conducted to survey manufacturers who made more than $500 annually. What's highlighted in these records? Information on employees, raw materials, expenses, the articles made, and the market value of such products. A similar census was taken again in 1832 to determine the effect foreign competition was having on domestic industry.

SLAVE SCHEDULES contain basic slave listings, complete with the market values of slaves purchased and information on any of the slaves' infirmaries such as blindness or deafness.

Remember, even if your property is not located in a "slave state," doesn't mean someone, sometime in the past didn't own and house slaves there. It wasn't uncommon for wealthy people throughout such Northern states as New Jersey, Pennsylvania, and even New York to own slaves prior to the Civil War. A quick perusal of slave schedules can be enlightening. They contain basic slave listings, market values of slaves and information on any slave infirmities such as blindness or deafness.

SEVERAL SUPPLEMENTAL SCHEDULES were taken from 1850 to 1880. These special census schedules offer a look at the agriculture, industry and society during those years. Depending on what your property has been used for in the past, one or all of these schedules may offer insightful facts about the property's long past.

Agriculture Schedules contain facts on owners' acreage (both improved and unimproved land), cash values of the farm, livestock, the amount of crops planted, and more.

Industry Schedules asked for this same type of information, but on manufacturers instead of farmers.

Social Statistics are helpful in other ways. They were gathered on each town, township and county's schools, libraries, newspapers churches, wages, residents.

THE INDEX TO INSTITUTIONS was taken from 1880 to 1920. It lists every American institution including schools, hospitals, orphans homes, poorhouses, jails, masonic homes, military forts, railroad and timber camps, fire stations, shaker communities, Indian reservations, or other types of institutions.

This special census is a wonderful resource to learning more about the rich and interesting segment of history of a property that has housed such an institution.

Organized by state, and then alphabetized by the name of the institution, the Index of Institutions gives the names of the institution, its location, number of residents, its usage and the volume, enumeration and district numbers as well as the page numbers of its location in the regular census record.

CROSS INDEX TO CITY STREETS of 1910 is most often used to find a property when a researcher can't find the name of the property owner for a given year. This index lists addresses for most larger cities. From it you can find out the name of the owner, at least at the time the census was formally taken.

- FEDERAL DIRECT TAX -

Nobody likes taxes. As unpopular as they are today, they were even more so during colonial times. In 1798, the United States tried, for the first time, to levy a tax on all citizens to finance a war between this country and France. The war may have never taken place, but those tax filings did. The Federal Direct Tax of 1798 was a tax assessed on buildings. This makes the records extremely valuable to any house genealogist. Some give remarkable descriptions on the building's materials, dimensions and height, barns and other outbuildings. As is the case with many older records, some offer only the bare minimum of information, others are more detailed.

Having learned what you can from local, state and federal land records, it is now time to turn to other sources to fill in the gaps about your home's history ...

WHERE TO FIND CENSUS RECORDS

In most cases you will not be able to view original census records. Most are now kept on microfilm and computer databases for review in branch offices throughout the nation. Many public university libraries, historical societies, archives and state repositories have the census records pertaining to their specific areas. Check these local contacts first. If you still need to view national archive records, contact the regional office nearest you:

NEW ENGLAND REGION
380 Trapelo Road
Waltham, MA 02154
(617) 647-8100
covers: Connecticut, Maine, Massachusetts, New Hampshire, Rhode Island and Vermont.

NORTHEAST REGION
Building 22 - MOT Bayonne
Bayonne, NJ 07002-5388
(201) 823-7252
covers: New Jersey, New York, Puerto Rico and the Virgin Islands

MID ATLANTIC REGION
9th and Market Streets, Room 1350
Philadelphia, Pa. 19107
(215)597-3000
covers: Delaware, Maryland, Pennsylvania, Virginia and West Virginia

SOUTHEAST REGION
1557 St. Joseph Avenue
East Point, GA 30344
(404) 763-7477
covers: Alabama, Georgia, Florida, Kentucky, Mississippi, North Carolina, South Carolina, and Tennessee

GREAT LAKES REGION
7358 South Pulaski Road
Chicago, IL 60629
(312) 581-7816
covers: Illinois, Indiana, Michigan, Minnesota, Ohio and Wisconsin

CENTRAL PLAINS REGION
2312 East Bannister Road
Kansas City, MO 64131
(816) 926-6272
covers: Iowa, Kansas, Missouri, and Nebraska

SOUTHEAST REGION
501 West Felix Street (building address)
P.O. Box 6216 (mailing address)
Fort Worth, TX 76115
(817) 334-5525
covers: Arkansas, Louisiana, New Mexico, Oklahoma and Texas

ROCKY MOUNTAIN REGION
Building 48, Denver Federal Center
Denver CO 80225
(303)236-0818
covers: Colorado, Montana, North Dakota, South Dakota, Utah, and
Wyoming.

PACIFIC SOUTHWEST REGION
24000 Avila Road (building address)
PO Box 6719 (mailing address)
Laguna Niguel CA 92677-6719
covers: Arizona, southern California and Nevada (Clark County)

PACIFIC SIERRA REGION
1000 Commodore Drive
San Bruno CA 94066
(415)876-9009

covers: Hawaii, Nevada, Northern California and the Pacific Ocean Region

PACIFIC NORTHWEST REGION
6125 Sand Pont Way NE
Seattle WA 98115
(206)526-6507
covers: Alaska, Idaho, Oregon, and Washington

HELPFUL GUIDES
FROM THE NATIONAL ARCHIVES

The National Archives offer many publications to help you locate the records you need to make your research as easy as possible. They may be ordered through any regional archive office:

* *Guide to Genealogical Research in the National Archives*

* *Using Records in the National Archives for Genealogical Research*

* *Guide to the National Archives of the United States*

* *Guide to Pre-Federal Records*

* *Microfilm Resources for Research in the National Archives*

* *Our Family, Our Town: Essays on Family and Local History*

CHAPTER FOUR:
Mining Local Historical Societies

A wonderful way to uncover little-known facts about your house, is to turn to the local historical society. Chances are, it's better equipped to track down historical data on individual properties within its research boundaries than any other source. After all, no one knows more about the history of the area where you live, than those who've dedicated their lives to studying and preserving it.

Historical society files are bulging with original records chronicling the lives of the people who built the community. Private papers, personal correspondence, business ledgers and biographies are just a few of the possessions prized by these organizations.

Individual facilities vary widely in the amount and depth of the formal research they offer. Some are staffed by paid archivists and librarians. Others are run solely on volunteer effort. It really doesn't matter whether your community's historical society is located in a large well-funded museum, or a forgotten broom closet in the basement of the town library. What matters most is its ability to provide the background materials you need — and its willingness to share its insight.

First time researchers often prefer to begin with smaller, less formal societies. Run by local history buffs, these facilities often seem friendlier and more willing to work with "amateur" researchers who may or may not know what they're looking for. It is not uncommon to have one of these helpers eagerly roll up their sleeves and join in the work of sifting through countless boxes and files looking for information.

Larger, more formal historic archives have much stricter rules. They seldom allow visitors to personally go through files. However, these organizations are generally more organized and know exactly where to locate specific materials. Run by experienced archivists, larger facilities also offer research services — for a price. A major drawback to using one of these centers is their intolerance for indiscriminate searches by visitors who wish to leisurely sift through records.

Whether large or small, walking through the doors of any historical society for the first time can be intimidating. There are literally thousands of books, documents and indexes to turn to for help. Where should you start? Here's just a sampling of the gems waiting to be uncovered:

- ACCOUNT LEDGERS -

To see what types of items previous owners bought to furnish, decorate and improve the house you now live in, check out the account ledgers of neighborhood drygoods and merchantile stores. These records feature detailed lists of transactions that may be used to verify any suspected improvements. For instance, a large lumber purchase may signify a room addition or major remodeling project.

Merchantile — **general all purpose housewares and grocery store**

- ARCHITECTURAL RECORDS -

Prior to the 1800s most ordinary homes were built without the use of blueprints. Instead, they used patterns handed down orally from generation to generation.

Homes built by wealthy and prominent citizens, on the other hand, were often designed by leading architects of the day. Remember: a house doesn't have to be a mansion to have once been occupied by a prominent citizen. Many seemingly simple homes by today's standards were one-of-a-kind masterpieces 100 years ago.

If architectural designs and sketches are available for your home, consider yourself lucky. They can provide a unique look at the property including the builder's "vision" for the project, not to mention floor plans and designs showing exactly what the house looked like from the very beginning.

- ATLASES & MAPS -

Atlases and maps have had many purposes throughout history. The earliest editions were compiled to record original land grant boundaries. Later, local municipalities used this forum to record growing boundaries and to show the placement of new roads and streets in burgeoning neighborhoods.

Atlas — a collection of maps bound in book form

Although most atlases and maps do not show specific buildings, they are still an important research tool for the house genealogist, since they do show how the plot relates to its environment (streams, hills). In many cases, they also specify land ownership.

Smaller boroughs and villages, however, often compiled detailed maps showing the placement of all streets and buildings. Some even featured illustrations of individual residences.

- BROADSIDES -

Getting the word out about meetings, sales and similar events wasn't easy before the advent of radio and television. Even newspapers offered limited help, since they were often distributed sporadically and were only purchased by the more educated classes.

Broadside — printed advertisements in poster form

The best way to let people know about upcoming events was to post printed announcements, or broadsides, on fences, trees and walls. Most were eventually destroyed by the elements or simply thrown away. But, thankfully, a handful of original printers' copies have been preserved by local historical societies. They are most useful when tracking down a sheriff or estate sales.

- DIRECTORIES -

When we want to locate a person or business today, we simply reach for the telephone book. What did people do before the telephone? Even early colonial communities of the 1700s solved this problem by compiling city directories which listed the names, addresses and occupations of all area residents. They are invaluable tools in tracing a house's occupancy.

Street indexes can be used to find unknown property owners for specific years. If your house isn't listed, don't despair. It probably wasn't built yet — an important clue in itself regarding its correct age.

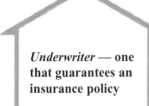

Underwriter — one that guarantees an insurance policy

-INSURANCE MAPS & RECORDS-

In the 1800s, the fire insurance business was booming. As it became harder for agents to personally inspect individual properties, the underwriters of these companies began to create insurance maps showing street layouts; the location of each building; its size and shape; as well as its approximate distance to the nearest hydrant. By 1924, there were more than 11,000 of these maps being used for writing insurance policies and distributing claims.

Fire insurance records, too, can help fill in the gaps of a house's history. When the discovery of a past fire is made for a house, these insurance records explain what damage occurred and give cost estimates for repairs.

- LOCAL HISTORIES -

In many instances, town histories were written to celebrate special events like centennial anniversaries. Others were written by local history buffs and even school children as history projects. Regardless of the author, or the reason for their creation, any local history is a wonderful resource for learning more about the people and places of your home town. Formal town histories, biographies of esteemed citizens and businesses as well as a run down of key events and local lore are often included.

During the Great Depression Era, the United States Department of the Interior made grants available to municipalities for use in conducting architectural surveys. These surveys describe in great detail specific house structures. Residences didn't have to be well-known or prominent in any way to be included. Some were chosen for their style, location or even size.

- MISCELLANEOUS RECORDS -

The families who've lived in your house more than likely generated a lot of family papers such as diaries, account ledgers and receipts.

As these paper collections accumulated, many were probably thrown out. But some of the more important documents may have been stored in trunks and boxes, forgotten for many years. Thankfully, many people have had the insight to donate these rediscovered collections to their local historical societies.

While the odds of finding some on your particular property are probably slim, it's always worth a look. The value of these types of records are tremendous to the house genealogist. Old diaries may mention building projects or other changes in the house, as well as give a day-to-day peek at the goings-on within the household. Family photographs offer a unique view of rooms and may help you to verify things you've surmised from other sources but were hard pressed to verify. Even average household receipts can hold clues to the furnishings of houses. Cumulated, each of these clues can create a panoramic view of your home during a specific time in its history.

- PHOTOGRAPHS & PRINTS -

Old photographs and prints may be some of the most fascinating documents you'll ever stumble across while researching your house.

Finding old photos is an exciting adventure. It may be the first time you've actually seen the way your house has looked in the past. It may look just the same. Or you might find yourself wondering if it is indeed the same house after all. With these old photos you'll have an in depth look not only of the house, but the landscaping as well.

Photos are also a great help in dating a house. If the attire of the people in the pictures doesn't give the era away, check for a photographer's seal in the corner. Then, look it up in the local directories for different periods to see when the photographer was in business. If all else fails, take the photo to an experienced photo historian. He should be able to tell the age of the print simply by the paper stock and developing method used.

When actual photographs are unavailable, you may have to rely on sketches. Sketching was a big hobby in the 1800s and early 1900s, especially among young ladies, who often practiced their drawing techniques by copying their family and home.

Don't be surprised to discover your house the feature of a postcard. Many local photographers had their best work reproduced into postcard form, which were later distributed.

-TELEPHONE HISTORIES -

If your house sports a small unrecognizable building either attached to the main structure, or in the side yard, or if it has odd room configuration near the kitchen and odd wiring, it may have been used as a telephone "central," transmission site for the neighborhood phone lines. During early phone days, they were located in every 10 houses or so. To find out if your house was among these centrals, check local telephone company history records stored at the historical society.

Central — **neighborhood transmission site for local telephone service**

CHAPTER FIVE:
Digging Through The Newspaper Morgue

At first glance, outdated newspapers often appear to be of little use to the homeowner's history search. Think again! From the earth-shattering to the mundane, newspapers are full of all kinds of interesting information. Local trivia abounds within their pages. Articles and columns give day-by-day accounts of a town's activities, as well as an overview of its people and businesses. Even old hot spots may be revealed.

That's not all. Older periodicals don't simply offer insight into a community. They can oftentimes lead to clues on more important aspects of your home's early history — if you read them carefully. Your house didn't necessarily have to be part of any "hot news" to be mentioned in the neighborhood newspaper.

Daily — a newspaper published every 24 hours

Advertisements. Wouldn't you be surprised to learn that your home sold for a mere $500 when it was first built? Real estate listings may reveal just that, and later selling prices too. Ads for new homes and other "for sale" notices may even give detailed descriptions of the property.

If your home was ever used as a place of business, other types of advertisements will tell you what kinds of services were offered there. At the very least, local sales ads can shed some light on the types of furnishings and decorations your house may have sported at one time or another.

Columns feature some of the most substantial clues regarding the community's houses and former residents. Neighborhood columns are loaded with useful information regarding influential people and the social events they attended, various meeting locations, as well as personal and public celebrations.

Some of the most useful finds, however, are hidden within the text of the everyday "gossip." The columnists who wrote them were some of the most well-informed people in the community. They knew every time someone broke ground for a new house, remodeled an old one, had trouble with a disreputable contractor, experienced drainage problems or even hung new curtains. And they weren't shy about telling everyone about it. That was their job.

Morgue — **collection of files and clippings in a newspaper office's research department**

Dig through these old columns. The time it takes just might be worth it, especially if you're lucky enough to stumble across some new and intriguing tidbits about your home. Besides, they're a lot of fun to read.

Legal Notices abound in both older and modern-day newspapers. The law requires public notices to be published for a variety of reasons: the sale of a house and other deed transfers, zoning changes to be announced, delinquent tax rolls and estate settlements. These notices can be especially helpful when court records have been lost or destroyed, since they can be used to reconstruct land sales, probate wills and tax rolls.

News Articles, too, may lead toward some unexpected avenues in your house-history journey. The most common may be information regarding a fire, a land dispute or even zoning requirement changes that have affected your property in the past. In more rare cases, you may learn about a murder which took place on the property or some other unsavory happening.

Obituaries are an excellent way to reconstruct lost title lines, especially in the case of an unknown owner who may have acquired the property by inheritance.

Personal Ads, especially those lost & found and for sale or for rent notices, may help you figure out what other uses your home may have had; for example if it was ever used as a boarding house or even a meeting hall of some sort.

Professional Notices may be used to help explain strange room configurations. Maybe the property was once divided for use as a lawyer, doctors or even accounting office.

Now that you know *what* to look for in old newspapers, *where* do you find these periodicals? Locating copies of outdated issues of neighborhood newspapers isn't very difficult in most communities. It's not uncommon to discover that the newspaper your ancestors read 50, 75 or even 100 years ago is the same one you have delivered to your doorstep today. If that's the case, a simple trip to the local library's microfilm department may yield all the old issues you'll ever need.

Periodical — printed material published at regular intervals

Tabloid — a digest-sized newspaper featuring news in condensed form

For access to every issue ever printed, a trip to the publisher's office may be necessary. Once there, you'll be led to the newspaper morgue. Most larger dailies have very organized research departments, complete with microfilmed issues indexed according to names, events and dates.

Smaller periodicals, including those free tabloids, don't usually have such official "morgues." Some don't even have any formal system of indexing. The best you can hope for in this case, is that the newspaper has copies bound annually for easy reference. Otherwise you may find yourself sitting in a back room, sifting through endless mounds of disorganized clippings.

What if the newspaper published during the time period you're researching has been out of print for years, or even decades? Check with the local historical society. They may either know the name of the publication, its publisher or have a few leftover copies in its files.

Weekly — a weekly issued newspaper

No matter where you turn for those old newspapers: the library, historical society, or its publisher, make an appointment. Some offices require researchers to know the exact issues and dates they are looking for and what type of information being sought. Most of the time, you'll be required to search individual issues yourself, but sometimes, you'll be required to tell the research department what you want and they'll find it and make copies for you. As with any type of research service, fees are usually involved.

Much of the information you come across will seem useless. Remember: even the most insignificant detail — when put together with other details — may lead to bigger, more important sources, and information you never anticipated.

FINDING ORIGINAL NEWSPAPERS

One way to determine which newspapers existed during the period in history being researched is to consult one of the following indexes:

American Bibliography: A Chronological Dictionary of All Books, Pamphlets and Periodic Publications Printed in the United States (1639-1820). Charles Evans

History and Bibliography of American Newspapers (1690-1820) Shoe String Press 1962

American Newspapers (1821-1936): A Union List of Files Available in the United States and Canada Kraus Reprint Corp.

A Checklist of American 18th Century Newspapers in the Library of Congress U.S. Printing Office 1912

Newspapers in Microform in the United States (1948-1983) Library of Congress 1984

Ayer Directory of Newspapers and Periodicals N.W. Ayer and Sons annual

Newspaper Indexes: A Location and Subject Guide for Research Scarecrow Press 1977-82

CHAPTER SIX:
Mining Memories

It's time to take your house genealogy search to the neighbors. Older residents may be able to tell you things about your home no one else knows. They often remember rumors involving the property and its former residents. At the very least, oral history sources can help you pinpoint dates to changes that have been made in recent years.

Getting neighbors to talk is easy. Elderly residents are eager to share their recollections. Just keep in mind that human memory is often faulty. It's not always easy to discern fact from fiction, especially when the truth is interspersed with bits of folklore. Misleading or misinterpreted facts can lead to bitter disappointment later on when you find out that your greatest discovery isn't true at all! One such scenario is common among historic homes located along the corridor once referred to as the Underground Railroad. It usually begins with a local legend that tells of fugitive slaves being hidden in area homes prior to the Civil War. Next, someone living in one of these houses discovers what appears to be a hidden room behind a basement wall. Bingo! Before anyone checks any further, the owner of the property is touted an instant amateur historian on local slave quarters by area journalists and schools. Unfortunately, further research by competent historians often unveils a much different story — much to the chagrin of the house's owner and the townspeople.

Folklore — **preserved tales**

Underground Railroad — **a system among anti-slavery people to aid fugitive slaves in their journey north.**

47

To check the validity of any story, double check its accuracy using both primary and secondary sources. Diaries of the people who lived in the house during the time period in question may mention the event. In the circumstance above, no mention may have signaled a red flag to the researcher. More in-depth property research may have concluded without questioning the inability of the room to have been used as a hidden slave quarters. How? Local records may prove that particular section of the house wasn't even built until years after the Civil War ended.

This is just one example of how accepting local legends too readily can lead to embarrassment. Avoid this trap. Always verify significant findings with more than one source.

Does this mean that oral history sources are completely unreliable? Not in the least. Despite the discrepancies they provide, they are useful in helping to fill gaps left in a house's history. Rarely totally accurate, oral histories are almost never totally wrong. Learning of unfamiliar family stories can lead to many exciting twists and turns in your journey.

-FINDING SOURCES -

At first it may seem nearly impossible to find people who know anything about your house. But, once you start digging, you'll discover that there is never a shortage of sources ready to share their insights. The easiest way to begin an oral history is to start with the previous owners and work backwards. Those who have actually lived in the house can tell you the most about it. They'll know exactly what the house was like when they first moved in, as well as any changes that occurred to the property and the neighborhood during the time they lived there.

Older residents are another good source, especially those who've lived in the neighborhood all of their lives. Many times these people are able to share stories about the people who lived in the house years ago, as well as local gossip. You may even learn when the maple tree in the front yard was planted.

One of the most reputable oral history sources is, of course, the local historian. They too, love to share their discoveries with those expressing genuine interest. Many have spent years researching the community, only to be left with a mere handful of fellow history buffs to share their amazing finds with.

One often overlooked place to find sources is the neighborhood church. Until fairly recently, most residents attended the closest church to their home — usually the one on the corner. Many of today's longtime congregants may remember things about the neighborhood and even your particular house from their youth. My next door neighbor learned the importance of mining the local church for information when she accidentally discovered that an elderly woman who sat a few pews behind her family each week had actually grown up in their house. As a matter-of-fact, the woman's grandparents built it. She shared many interesting facts about the house with my friends that no one else could have known. This has added a unique element to the formal history of their house.

-CONDUCTING THE INTERVIEW -

Finding oral history sources is the easy part. Gleaning the right information from them takes a little more skill. The first step to a successful interview is doing your homework. Before sitting down to chat, find out whatever you can about your interviewee, and his/her relationship to your house. If, for example, he lived there (or nearby) as a toddler, the odds aren't great that he'll remember much firsthand. But, if he has possession of pictures taken of the fireplace at Christmastime, you've got something to work with.

Let your subject know in advance what topics you'll be discussing. Asking someone to tell you "everything you know about the old James' place," doesn't leave you with much direction for questioning. Instead, ask about specific time periods, people and events.

Set a time and place for your interview. Conducting your questioning in the house itself may help to spark additional memories.

On the day of the interview, spend time chatting informally for awhile. This will help to put your subject (and yourself) at ease. Keep it casual. Remember, you're trying to learn more about your house, not win a Pulitzer Prize for your amazing interviewing skills. If it's not too uncomfortable for either of you, use a small tape machine to record your conversation. This will help free you from your notepad and allow you to pay better attention to your interview subject. Never rely totally on the recorder, though. Hand written notes are useful, especially if anything happens to the tape.

One problem that often arises in this type of interview setting is allowing the conversation to wander aimlessly off track. When this happens (and it will), take charge. Casually steer the focus of your conversation back to the main subject — your house. A good way to do this is to concentrate on details.

Moving too quickly off the subject can also be a danger. Patience is also a key. What may appear to be a long-winded story about your interviewee's childhood friendship with the girl who lived in your home in the 1940's, may lead to an interesting story about the late night shenanigans the two shared sneaking out the back alleyway — an alleyway you may have never known existed.

The lessons to be learned here is to be patient, while exhibiting some control over the interview. And never let your guard down. Pay attention. Follow up all unusual leads with a barrage of additional questions. You'll be surprised at what you find out. Whenever possible, ask for some type of documentation: letters; a diary; family photos; or even a child's drawing.

After the interview, take time right away to transcribe those scribbled notes while the conversation is still fresh in your mind. Listen carefully to your interview tapes, marking off important sections. Now's not the time to be shy about calling to verify things you don't understand or need elaboration on.

Within a day or two of each interview, send your subjects a quick thank you note or small gift of appreciation. After all, these people didn't have to take the time to sit down and answer your questions. Pay them the common courtesy of expressing your thanks.

QUESTIONS TO ASK

You've found a source or two with firsthand knowledge about your house. Now what? Here are a few questions to get you started:

Who has lived in the house? What was their lifestyle like? Were they rich or poor? Laborers or businessmen?

What key events happened in this house? Were there any fires? Crimes? Deaths?

Have any major improvements or additions been made? When? Who did the work: owners or a hired contractor?

Do you remember any old-fashioned fixtures such as an outhouse or well? Where was it located? When was it taken down? Has the house always had indoor plumbing and electricity? If not, when was it added?

What colors has it been painted? Was there ever siding or brick facing?

What about hardwood floors? Do you remember any? When were they added or removed?

Know of any strange stories or rumors regarding the house? Has it ever been haunted?

How about fireplaces? Were there ever any? In which rooms? What did they look like?

Do you have any old pictures of the house, either inside or outside?

Is there anyone else that you know of who might be able to answer some questions about the house? Who? Where can I find him/her?

SECTION II:

FROM THE OUTSIDE LOOKING IN

SECTION II
Introduction

If only these walls could talk ... they can! Ok, so your house isn't going to yell out its construction date in a loud bellowing voice, but it can tell you when it was built —in its own way.

Like people, houses undergo a lot of changes as they age. Little by little, technological advances creep into our lives, and our houses. Privies are replaced with indoor plumbing. Gas powered lamps make room for electrical outlets. Even everyday repairs can have a lasting impact on a house's overall structural history.

Its physical evidence can tell you as much about its history as the formal documentation that you've already gathered. Imagine something as ordinary as a nail unlocking the secrets to your home. It can. If you know the types of nails used during specific construction periods.

In Section II, you'll learn how to gather clues to your home's unique architectural characteristics and structural variations. From the attic to the basement; the flooring to the ceiling; to the windows and doors, you'll discover key clues to your house's past by learning to interpret even the most irrelevant clues.

Ready to get started on this new avenue in your search? First, ask your house a question. Then, listen carefully. You just might get an answer.

Colonial

Spanish Revival

CHAPTER SEVEN
Basic House Styles

Houses certainly have changed over the years. The first American settlers may have been happy living in hand-hewn cabins, but not for long. Better tools and construction methods soon made these simple shelters obsolete.

When the wealth of the colonies began to grow, so did the homes of its inhabitants. Suddenly, even the one room frame houses which had replaced those first cabins weren't enough. The aristocracy of the 1700s wanted luxury. They wanted to reconstruct the best mansions and palaces of Europe right here in their new homeland, so the colonists began importing architects and materials from oversees.

Meanwhile, the average American was upgrading too, albeit on a smaller scale. As the upper class worked to outdo one another with their grand estates, the middle class settled for the charm of simple colonial styles. But, by the 1800s even they were caught up in the building frenzy. Anxious to expand their families and start enjoying the benefits of larger houses, homeowners rang in the Victorian Era by building roomier houses featuring romantic towers, rounded arched windows and balconies.

As interests and tastes change, so do houses. Today's historic homeowner may discover that his house doesn't fit one single style, but is a mix of popular features from several different construction periods. For instance, the main structure may be colonial, but feature Victorian gables and Greek Revival pillars. This can make pinpointing a house's authentic style frustrating.

That's why you need to familiarize yourself with basic American house styles. Knowing what style (or styles) your house resembles, will point you to other construction and structural clues in dating your historic home. Here's a quick rundown of the most basic house styles:

— COLONIAL —
(1600-1820)

The first American homes were primitive thatched sheds or log cabins. Built out of necessity, these early shelters were sparse, to say the least. Most had virtually no style, and offered little in domestic comfort. Cramped and simple, these one room structures had a fireplace for cooking and heating, a loft for sleeping, and usually just a dirt floor.

The colonists lived this way for quite awhile. But, once their communities were on solid footing they began to upgrade. As soon as the proper tools and better construction methods were available, the primitive housing the settlers started off with gave way to a more charming colonial style which incorporated the origins and tastes from their homelands.

The most popular was a two-story dwelling built on a frame with jointed timbers. Simple in style and sturdy in its construction, the newer design offered more comfort and privacy. The second story provided separate sleeping quarters away from the community area. Domestic chores grew easier too, with the addition of a large eight to twelve foot wide central chimney.

As the average citizen basked in all this extra space, the homes of the prominent colonist continued to grow more and more elaborate. The overly adorned Georgian mansion (based on the palaces of the Italian Renaissance) was the most popular among the high society group.

Even after the Revolutionary War, when everyone wanted to forget everything British, (including the overstated Georgian house), the colonial aristocracy wouldn't give up their showplaces. They did, however, pare down the Georgian ornamentation with a more austere version known best as The Federal.

Classic and simple from the outside, its interior was no less elegant. Large oval rooms were surrounded by winding staircases and decorative mantels.

As you can see, the styles built during the colonial period are endless, depending a great deal on the builder's personal tastes, and financial status, and climate of the area where the house was built.

For instance, Southern Georgian homes often sported a separate kitchen because of the blistering heat of the summer months, while New England homes were built to accommodate the regions frigid winters by connecting the outbuildings to the main house using hallways and enclosed porches.

For this reason, the colonial styles listed below may vary somewhat from region to region. Their main features, however, should be similar in design:

- SPANISH COLONIAL -
(1565-1800)

Most popular from 1565 to 1800 in warm-weather climates, the *Spanish Colonial* is a long and low one-story abode, constructed of timber and masonry. Adobe was preferred when available. The roof was made of layered horizontal logs laid across the top walls and covered with sticks, clay and/or tiles.

- EARLY AMERICAN -
(1603-1800)

The Early American (1603-1800) was built with an emphasis on survival. A boxy, plain looking house, this early dwelling was built to resemble the medieval English styles most familiar to the settlers, with special adaptions made to accommodate the harsh winters of North America. With a steep pitched roof, this two-room house featured a master bedroom and cooking/eating area on the ground floor, with an attic-like bedroom space above.

Adobe — bricks made of sun-dried earth and straw

- THE DUTCH COLONIAL -
(1625-1820)

Dutch Colonials were most popular from 1625-1820. A timber framed house, it is H shaped and often features a stone or brick facade. One and a half stories high, the Dutch Colonial is best recognized for its gambrel two-pitched roof and overhanging eaves. It has usable living space on both floors. The ceilings are made of smoothed beams. Its most recognizable feature is the classic Dutch door, which is divided horizontally, allowing the top and bottom halves to be opened independently.

- THE GEORGIAN STYLE -

The elaborate *Georgian* house, is based on the Italian Renaissance and is made of clapboard and masonry construction. Formality and symmetry is essential to this style. It stands two stories tall, and is topped with a gabled roof and two pairs of chimneys. The first floor features the house's "hallmark," an elaborate doorway flanked by evenly spaced windows and large columns. Once inside, a central hall is flanked by pairs of rooms on either side. Wall coverings included paneling, plastered crown moldings and wainscoting. Sliding sash windows with multiple panes of glass were common, as were classic pilasters with adorned corners and cornice decorations.

- THE FEDERAL -
(mid 1800s)

The Federal (mid-1800s), was classically understated in comparison to its garish counterpart. A simplified version of the Georgian, it stood 2 to 3 stories high and was built in the shape of a square or rectangle in clapboard or brick. A plain and simple exterior was framed by a flattish roof with narrow windows. A

Clapboard — wood siding

fan sash was often found over the doorway with flanking sidelights. Elegant in every manner, the Federal featured decorated mantels, cornices and ceilings, as well as plaster ornamentations of delicate cures, rosettes, swags and rosebuds throughout. It also contained a brand new feature to American homes of the time: built-in closets.

- VICTORIAN -
(1800-1900)

The Victorian Age was a boon for homebuilding. Virtually overnight millions of new structures sprung up in almost every community.

The Industrial Revolution allowed everyone to live stylishly. Machines suddenly could mass produce ready-made fixtures and appliances at a fraction of the cost of hiring artisans and craftsman to hand-mold woodwork and decorations.

As more choices became available, redecorating became the popular thing to do. For the first time, the very essence of a home could be changed at little cost, with the turn of a catalogue page. The spirit of Victorian architecture was a willingness to try anything. Rooms were added onto houses at various and often strange angles, jutting out from the front, back and sides. Porches resembling Greek porticos were numerous, often connecting newly built sections with older ones. Stained glass sashes became the house's focal point. These "picture windows" were all the vogue. This craving for variety led to dozens of building variations in the Victorian house style. Here are just a few:

- THE GREEK REVIVAL -
(1820-1860s)

The Greek Revival period gained prominence in 1820 and held its popularity through the 1860's. Like most homes built during the Victorian Era, there was quite a bit of latitude exercised in constructing this particular style. From the austere temple-like fortress, to the simple Colonial replica with a massive square porch over the front door, the Greek Revival came in almost every shape and size imaginable. The days of formality were set aside. These houses took on a life of their own.

Although the exterior featured a gable-end facade and large pillars, the interiors were much simpler. There were few moldings. Even the once sought-after cornices and decorations were sparse. Walls were made of plaster. Doorways set back a foot or more from the plane, accented by marble or grained doors.

- THE GOTHIC REVIVAL -
(mid 1800s)

The Gothic Revival of the mid 1800s owes much of its success to the circular saw, which allowed carpenters to shape woods and create elaborate gingerbread designs for the first time.

Reminiscent of the Medieval Gothic style, the American Gothic freely used Italian, French, Tudor and Oriental influence in its design.

Barge board — board affixed to the rooftop to hide carpentry

Veranda — roofed open portico attached to a building

Built mostly of wood, its V-shape adds to the Gothic's vertical emphasis. From its pointed archways to the gabled rooftops, every aspect of the Gothic's construction lends itself to an appearance of "reaching for the stars."

Barge boards were used to outline the gabled front. An all-embracing veranda often gathered the wings that stuck out from the main structure.

Inside, the floor plan was, for the first time, asymmetrical, with an L-plan.

- THE AMERICAN BRACKET -
(Late 1800s)

In the latter half of the 19th century, the *Italiante* dominated the building scene. This simple, boxlike house resembled an Italian villa. Standing two to three stories high, it usually featured a square cupola, although round ones were not uncommon. Its wide overhanging roof is supported by wooden brackets. Hence the nickname, "The American Bracket."

High Victorian Gothic

Octogonal

(Courtesy The Old York Road Historical Society)
Second Empire

(Courtesy The Old York Road Historical Society)
Queen Anne

The charm of its towers, bay windows and balconies made this house a favorite style throughout the Civil War period. Porches too were an absolute must.

Instead of the sashes and sidelights of the previous styles, The *Italiante* was the first to use glass in its double entrance doors. These tall, narrow windows had rounded tops.

Cupola — small structure built on top of roof

- THE OCTAGONAL -
(1850-1865)

The unusual configuration of the eight-sided *Octagonal* house was short-lived. Popular between 1850-1865, this two-story cupola house was designed by Orson S. Fowler, a phrenologist who believed that circular structures were a healthy and efficient form of building since they allowed for maximum air flow throughout the rooms. However, the structure did not hold up to time and use like other styles.

As unique as the exterior, its strange design created even more peculiar room proportions inside. While larger living areas often took on a more rectangular shape, smaller rooms and closets featured triangular layouts and off-beat corners.

- THE SECOND EMPIRE -
(1860-1890)

The octagonal fad made way for the *Second Empire* house, which reigned from 1860-1890. Identified by its double-pitched Mansard Roof, this three-story rectangular house fit perfectly into the narrow lots of nineteenth century urban America.

Its characteristic roof slopes from two peaks at an almost flat pitch, becoming vertical at the decorated eaves. Most Empires contain dormers. Double entry doors open into an impressive interior, with high ceilings and tall arched windows.

- THE QUEEN ANNE -
(1870-1900)

The *Queen Anne* style of the late nineteenth century (1870-1900), blended the best of the Gothic and Renaissance elements. Its structural variation and decoration was borrowed from every possible source known. This eclectic style blends roof lines, dormers, gables and multiple chimneys to create a complex irregular roof with cross gables. Bay windows and porches are found in the front. A front facing gable finishes off the exterior's ensemble.

Inside, a myriad of different materials and textures were also used, as were bold and rich colors.

- SHINGLE STYLE -
(1880-1900)

Most popular in the western territories, the *Shingle Style* house of the 1880s and 1890s was a large, comfortable abode.

Gable — triangular end of building from cornice to eave ridge

Palladian — a three-part window: tall center window, flanked by two smaller ones

A simple, unpainted style with siding and gabled roofs, this two or three story house featured mixed roof lines, small overhangs, porches and Palladian windows. Treatments were simple as were adornments.

- MODERN -
(1900 - present)

The twentieth century has been a time of great improvement in home building. New nails and cutting tools revolutionized construction methods. As houses were wired for electricity, central heating and were fitted for plumbing, standardization became the rule.

Steel frames began to replace wooden ones in large formal buildings. Natural materials made a comeback as consumers once again realized the value of high-quality handmade goods.

From 1908 to 1940, pre-fab house kits were the rage. No longer forced to hire an architect and builder, homeowners could order practically any house they wanted from a catalogue and have it delivered, nearly ready-made.

Styles were comfortable and simple. Long, low open rooms were common, as were center hallways. Buildings generally were shaped in an L or a T during this construction era.

Despite the building changes and improvements taking place, bringing back the old was also in vogue as many chose to build replicas of earlier colonial styles.

Two of the most original house styles of the early 20th century were the Bungalow and the Prairie School.

- THE BUNGALOW -
(1900-1930)

The Bungalow, had a thirty-year building stint, which ran from 1900-1930. Although there are many variations of this simple style, its most unmistakable features are a gentle sloping roof, dormers, small porch and exposed rafters and ridge poles.

Designed after the Indian bungalow, this 1½ story house is small and simple. The front door leads directly into the living room. Amazingly, however, most feature an oversized stone fireplace. Dormers offer more usable sleeping space upstairs.

- THE PRAIRIE SCHOOL -
(1900-1920)

The Prairie School (1900-1920), was designed by Frank Lloyd Wright. Shaped horizontally, this low-to-the ground house features two stories on the main building, with a one story wing adjacent, creating an L-shaped structure.

Made of brick and wood, and covered with masonry and stucco, the exterior also features a broad overhang and a myriad of terraces, balconies and exterior walkways, giving this house a unique indoor-outdoor feel.

Inside, there are few rooms, although each is generally quite large and open. The interior space is divided, not by doors, but rather, by large archways.

As you can see, there are quite a few varieties of styles of houses built during our country's long history. Even when a style is unmistakable, you may find elements of other styles hidden within its interior, especially in the historic house which has survived endless renovations and improvements over the years.

To correctly chronicle the building history of your home, it's time to turn to its construction methods for further clues...

THE COLONIAL ERA

Primitive	— Prior to 1700
Early American	— 1700-1720
Georgian	— 1720-1780
Federal	— 1780-1800

THE VICTORIAN ERA

Greek Revival	— 1820-1840
Gothic Revival	— 1836-1900
Romanesque	— 1850-1890

CHAPTER EIGHT:
Construction Clues ...

Some of the most important discoveries you'll make about your house (and its history), will come from its construction clues. After all, a copy of a building permit can only tell you building "plans." It'll take physical evidence from the house itself to show you what was done — and how.

There are a lot of things to keep in mind when looking for construction clues. As you investigate the nooks and crannies of your old house, you'll want to keep these questions in mind:

Does the physical evidence I've found seem to be original, or has it been changed over the years? If the house you're researching is more than 15-20 years old, the odds are it has undergone quite a few changes since it was built. Your job as a house genealogist is to look beyond your initial findings to figure out whether the physical evidence you've uncovered is original to the property, or just part of its "lineage."

How has style and fashion influenced my house? No house stays the same. The fact is, styles and tastes change. Large pane windows are replaced by smaller, double-hung insulated ones; stucco is covered by siding; even closets are torn out or added depending on the style of the times.

The most obvious changes most historic homes undergo is due to technological advances. No matter how much you revel in your home's historic flavor, aren't you glad it now has hot and cold running water, electric lights and that all-important bathroom?

Don't discount the changes these kind of technological wonders may have had on your house. A discovery as simple as learning that your laundry room once was a mud room that housed dirty boots and coats, will give you a better idea of how your house was used in the past.

Does my house appear to have been built all at once, or in stages? Before the 1800s, houses weren't built all at once like they are today, but room-by-room in order to meet a growing family's needs. How can you tell if your house was one of these sectional palaces? One trick is to measure the bays on either side of the windows. If they don't match, it could be a sign that your house has been expanded one, two or even more times.

Answering these few initial questions won't tell you everything there is to know about your house, but it's a good place to start. Now, let's look at a few of the best places to begin searching for construction clues:

-FOUNDATION-

Considering the fact that it's the first part of any structure to be built, it makes sense that a building's foundation may be the best source to dating it. What's the best way to date a house's foundation? Start with the material it's made of:

STONE

Stone has been used to lay foundations since the first settlers built their homes in the colonies. The kind of stones used in building has varied depending on what was available at the time. The fieldstone picked from the farmer's fields was most commonly used for northern farmhouses. In contrast, a house built with easy access to a quarry might have a higher-grade foundation made of limestone, sandstone, granite or even marble.

One rule of thumb regarding stone foundations is: the thicker the wall, the older the house. Believe it or not, people aren't kidding when they say they don't build houses like they used to. They don't. Beginning in the 19th century, many builders opted to replace the thick outer walls (and some interior ones for that matter), that were meant to stand for generations, with less expensive thinner skeletons.

BRICK

Brick too, has almost always been used in home building. It's solid, clean-looking and long lasting, all attributes a good builder looks for in construction materials. Don't let the fact that brick has been used for centuries intimidate you. There are still ways to date it. The first thing to remember is that bricks were made by hand until the mid-1800s. These early versions are easy to spot since they are full of irregularities. Their size, shape and texture are all different, leaving them ill-uniformed. By 1850, machine-made bricks of consistent shape and texture were the norm. These can be detected by their texture, since they feel more like concrete than brick.

Size also changed with the times. Before 1830, brick had no standard size. From the mid 1800s to the early part of this century, the average brick was small, measuring a mere 1½" high. Today's bricks are much larger, measuring a whopping 2½" h x 4" w in comparison.

Color, too, is a good indication of a brick's true age. The machine-made ones we're used to are almost always reddish in tint. That wasn't so in the past. Older bricks (especially those made by the early Dutch settlers), weren't usually red. Many were pink, orange and even yellow.

Another way to date brick is by its bond, or the way it's headers and footers are arranged in the wall.

PITFALL ...

If you find burnt timbers in your home, don't automatically assume there was a fire in your house's history. Those burnt logs may have been a result of the slash and burn method used to clear forests in early colonial days.

In the slash and burn method, a small brush fire was made at the base of a large tree, which scorched the trunk and lower branches. The injured tree was later more easily removed since it was dry and dying, and some of the wood cut from the tree may still show signs of the fire.

THE ENGLISH BOND was most popular in the 17th century. This style alternated a header and stretcher.

THE FLEMISH BOND, popular in the 18th century featured a row of headers, then a row of stretchers.

THE COMMON BOND (hence its name), is the most common method of bricklaying. It's construction is made of all stretchers. It gained popularity since it was introduced in the 19th century, and is still used today.

CONCRETE BLOCK
Concrete block was introduced around 1875. Poured concrete, however, did not become a popular building material until fairly recently.

FALSE STONE
False stone became popular in the early 1900s once machines became available to mass produce them. How can you tell if your foundation is built with these fake stones? False stones are easy to spot under close scrutiny. They all look alike and feel like concrete to the touch.

-MASONRY-

The brickwork of a house can be bonded two ways: dry-laid or mortared. Dry-laid is best, since it prevents fungi, insects and cracks by allowing water to drain. To tell if a wall has been dry-laid look for:

* stones that rest on two fellows
* vertical joints that do not line up
* a thick base

Despite the apparent advantages of dry-laying a foundation, mortar has always been the most common way to bond a wall. The age of a wall's mortar can be detected by the materials used in making it. For example, the early settlers used a mud and clay mixture that was strengthened by using hog's hair.

In the 1700s many builders (especially those along the shoreline), began using crushed oyster shells in lime for their mortar.

But, by 1819, pulverized limestone was all the rage, until, that is, a stronger portland cement made of lime, silica, iron oxide and alumnia was patented in 1871. A variation of this mortar is still used today.

-TIMBER-

Since the first settlers began clearing America's dense forests in the 1600s, more houses have been constructed using wood than any other material. The type of wood used to frame a house is your first indication to its age. Most of the early settlers liked to use woods they were familiar with from home. For

Hewn — wood squared by hand with a broadax

instance, Englishman preferred oak; Dutch, pine and Germans, fir trees. You may be able to get a good idea of the time period in which your house was built simply by connecting the wood used to build it with specific immigration periods.

Joist — a horizontal support beam

Now, take a good look at the wood beams and joists in your cellar and attic. Does it appear to be hand-hewn? Do the beams sport saw marks? What do they look like?

Hand hewn timbers are the oldest, dating back to the 1600 and 1700s. They are characterized by shallow slashes in a diagonal direction made by the broadax as it was being squared into usable logs. In some early homes, the joists and rafters were only hewn on one side, with the tree bark left on the other.

English Bond Brick Style

Flemish Bond Brick Style

Common Bond Brick Style

Zig Zag Common Bond Brick Style

Split wood was popular in the 18th century as better and better tools became available. Its surface often appears "splintered."

Sawed wood came into wide-spread use in the 1800s, although some of the wealthier builders before then had access to them. As is the case with most building styles and tools, saws changed over the years too. Here's a quick guide to the most common saw marks used during specific time periods:

The pit saw was most popular in the 1600 and 1700s. It makes wide-spaced marks in the wood.

The sash saw was used in the 18th and 19th centuries. It sports deep wide, consistent spaced marks that run perpendicular.

Circular saws came into vogue during the mid-1800s. Its marks are recognized by their crescent shape.

Band saws of the late 1800s and early 1900s sport closely spaced parallel marks that are often found in standard-sized lumber.

-FRAMING-

How a house is framed may tell you even more about the time period in which it was built since almost every builder adhered to certain "building standards" during specific periods in history.

CLUE ...
The United States suffered a severe chestnut blight in the 1840s, followed by another in the 1900s. Therefore, if you discover chestnut studs and joists in an older home, you can usually surmise that your home was built sometime between 1840 and the late 1860s.

Almost all 17th century homes were built using a plank-framing design. In it, thick vertical planks, which functioned as studs, were set 2" apart (using oak pegs, not nails), on the exterior sill or plate. Gaps around the sill were filled with clay and straw.

By the 18th century, the exterior walls were being built by centering one stud to the center of the next, with the top and bottom joined with mortise and tenon joints.

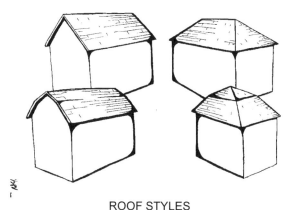

ROOF STYLES
(Top left): Gable Roof; (Bottom left): Gambrel Roof;
(Top right): Hip Roof; (Bottom right): Mansard Roof

During the 19th century house framing went through a transitional period as saw mills became available, making lumber more readily available.   Balloon framing revolutionized the two-story house construction during the mid-1880s. Standard sizes of lumber were used for the first time, enabling builders to use studs that were two stories high, which eliminated the use of beams for support. This method was used almost universally until platform framing replaced it early in the 20th century, when builders began constructing one floor on top of the other.

-ROOFS-

Although dating the materials used to build your roof are important, they can provide a false sense of timing since few homes (if any) still have their original roof covering. So how can you tell how old your roof is? First, check the pitch. A steep pitch that hangs over the windows of a 1 ½ story house is of pre-1770. After 1770, the pitch (which isn't as steep as its predecessor), ends about 2 1/2-3 feet above the window heads.

Next, look for evidence of the materials that have been used on your house's roof in the past. Then compare it to these general building guidelines:

1600s   — thatched from straw (this will be undetectable)
1700s   — pine or cedar logs cut into 2 foot shingle sections

early 1800s	— sawn "splintered" shingles
mid 1800s	— first composition roofing made of cloth, felt and paper soaked in tar
late 1800s	— tin
general 1800s	— slate shingles/ wood shingles
1900s	— asphalt

-WINDOWS-

There are several key identifying characteristics to dating a house's windows. While the odds that your house still has its original windows are somewhat rare, you may find one or two still remaining in places where windows are rarely replaced, like the attic or dormers.

When checking windows for clues to their age, you'll want to take a good look at the glass. The oldest windows are made of hand blown glass full of imperfections such as curved waves and bubbles, making it less than see through.

Since stained glass wasn't generally used before the 1800s this type of window would indicate at least a 19th century installation. Single pane picture windows are indicative of a post-WWII installation. Since both of these windows (as were other styles), were often added to older homes during renovation projects, great care should be exercised when using windows as a judge for dating a home.

A good way to figure out how old the windows in your house are is to count its panes. Common configurations of the 1700s includes 12 panes over eight panes; nine panes over nine panes and nine panes over six panes. As the end of the century approached, many builders opted to use a six over six pane window. By the mid 1800s, a simpler two panes over two panes was most common. It was replaced a few years later by one pane over one pane, the most common configuration in use today.

-DOORS-

Since changing a front door is an easy and relatively inexpensive way to modernize the look of an older home, few historic properties still sport their original doors. That doesn't mean its wood setting and transom details won't offer some clues to dating the door frame, thus, your whole house.

Transoms (the panes across the top of the door), are an excellent way to date a doorway. Transoms were introduced in the 18th century to provide light into the foyer without risking security. Most of the early ones were simple rows of small windows. As houses became more elaborate, so did their entryways. By the end of the century they had evolved into a fanlight design. Sidelights were then added, and by the 1820s the entire entryway of many homes became an elaborate showplace of woodwork and windows. Rectangular transoms and sidelights were soon all the rage. They remained popular for about 20 years, until the pointed arch and u-shaped transom came into vogue. By the 20th century, there were so many styles being used that it became impossible to date any of these doorways using the transoms and wood-work as a guide.

Flue — an enclosed channel in a chimney which directs smoke and heat

-CHIMNEYS-

Your home's chimney(s) can tell you a lot about the age of the structure. First count them. One or two is the most common. More than two may indicate an addition was made to the property at one time.

Transom — a window or light above a door (usually an entryway door)

Next, check the placement of the chimney(s). A center chimney is a good sign that your house dates back to the 17th or 18th century. If it is off center, it may have been built as late as the 19th century.

Early houses from the 1600s and 1700s often featured big chimneys with several flues which were used to heat several rooms.

Two interior chimneys located at either end of the house probably dates back to the 18th or 19th century.

A beehive oven (an exterior oven with indoor access) was common in the late 1700s and early 1800s, except in the country's southern states, where the oven was most often built in the yard, to keep the heat and fire danger away from the house.

Now that you've used these major exterior clues for evidence to properly date the structure, let's take a look inside to learn more ...

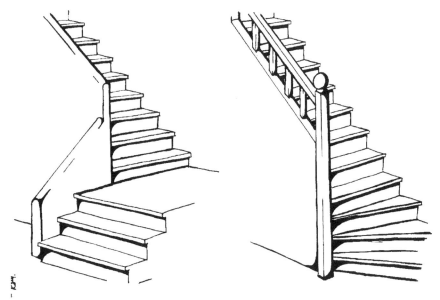

Georgian Style staircase - mid 1700s

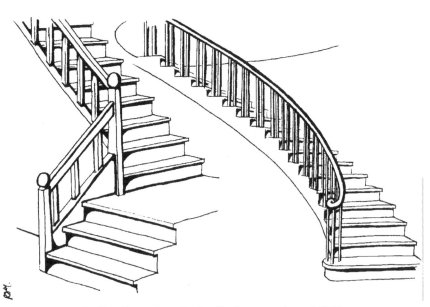

(left): Georgian Style Staircase - late 1700s
(right): Federal Style Staircase - early 1700s

CHAPTER NINE:
Upstairs/Downstairs

What attracts us to a particular home? Maybe the unique walk-in fireplace that made you fall in love with your Colonial. Or, it may have been the quaint gingerbread that drew you to that old Victorian. It's these details that old house lovers find enchanting. Now, let's step beyond the threshold of your own home and take a good look at the details that make it unique.

The moldings, fireplaces and stairwells may hold potential clues to your house's history. They probably won't be able to pinpoint the exact date that it was built, but they can be used in conjunction with the information you've already uncovered, to add a few chapters to your house's special story.

- MOLDINGS -

The purpose of molding is simple — to join sections of a room together (the floor to the wall, ceiling to the wall, etc). These strips of wood can be very plain or very ornamental, depending on the style of the time in which it was installed.

Cornice — **piece of top molding that crowns a wall**

The best way to date the mold-ings of a house is to figure out what style it is and whether or not it matches the style of your home's original architecture.

EARLY AMERICAN: The first thing to remember when investigating the moldings in an early American house is that few homes even sported any such ornamentation until the 1800s. When moldings were used prior to that date, they were generally simple versions, made of crude pieces of wood fitted together.

In the 1700s pine was the most popular wood used for moldings since it was an easier wood to plane by hand. Although harder woods did come into fashion by the end of the century as better hand tools and powered planing machines became available, most 18th century moldings are still characterized by:

* Circular composition — almost all moldings in this century was planed using a circular arc.
* Shape — broad, flat and low moldings were most common to this century

As homes became more and more elaborate in the 1800s, so did their interior moldings and wood-work. Better machinery was intro-duced, making moldings easier and cheaper to reproduce. They were also lighter, making them easier to install. But, the biggest change was in the way they looked. 19th century moldings featured a more ellipse of curves rather than circles. Plaster moldings also became popular during this time.

Planing — to smooth or shape a piece of wood

Modern moldings (post 1900) are usually just replicas of earlier styles. The best way to determine whether the molding in your home is original or a reproduction is to determine if it was made by early (and often cruder) machinery or today's high powered and "perfect" machines.

- STAIRWELLS -

Balusters — a rail support

Newel — the post at the foot and top of a stairway

Stairwells may have been changed more than any other house feature in the early days of construction. During the 1700s alone a variety of different styles took precedence. The type of wood your staircase is made from is also a very important clue in dating it. Staircases of the 18th century featured mostly oak handrails and newel posts, attached using pine balusters. By the

19th century, cherry was most popular for the entire staircases, followed by walnut during the second empire building resurgence.

The placement of your staircase is also important. In the early to mid part of the 18th century, staircases wound around the corner of the fireplaces, giving an elegant spiral look to even the plainest home. Wainscotting was common to the handrail until the latter part of the century when a partially paneled wall was introduced along the wall leading to an open balustrade above. In the last remaining years of the 1700s, plaster and baseboard prevailed.

Although the main staircase was almost always near the front entrance, its placement has changed many times over the years. By 1820 stair place-ment varied in accordance

CLUE ...
Does your cornice molding suddenly stop in a corner, instead of making the turn along the wall? The odds are, the wall without the cornice was added later.

to the house's style. For instance, in a Georgian style house the stair-case is found against the wall in the center hall (aristocratic homes featured central staircases), while the Federal featured an elliptical staircase placed on one side of a center hall. The Greek revival style featured a side hall entrance, which placed the staircase inside the outside wall for the first time.

- FIREPLACES -

More than any other interior feature, fireplaces may offer the best clues to a house's age; mainly because fireplaces and chimneys were difficult to take out, leaving lasting clues to a house's original age and structure. Even when a fireplace may have been removed (or in many cases covered over with brick or wallboard), chances are that some evidence such as a base in the basement or chimney in the attic near the roof, remains, proving that it once existed.

A good rule of thumb when dating a chimney is: the bigger it is, the older it is. Early fireplaces were working spaces. They were generally large (often 3 to 5 feet deep) and located in the center of the house.

By the mid 1700s, flues were being added to scaled down versions of the massive stone fireplaces of earlier years. They were then moved from the central part of the house to the corner of the room. But by the latter part of the century they were put front and center once again. By the century's end, coal was being introduced as a major heat source, making fireplaces obsolete virtually overnight. In the 1800s many homeowners closed up the fireplace altogether and cut flues in the chimney to make way for these newer coal stoves.

Mantel — **the finishing around a fireplace**

Mantels, on the other hand, remained popular, even long after the actual working fireplaces were boarded up or removed.

Stone hearths were most common in the early Colonial , with paneled mantels from floor to ceiling.

The Federal style of the 1800s introduced a wall division using a horizontal chair rail, followed by a solid mantel that stood alone (often with no fireplace) during the Greek Revival of the mid-1800s. Arched mantels made of marble were often found in wealthier homes.

By the time the Victorian era rang in, mantels had become quite elaborate, featuring delicate and intricate carvings. These gave way once again to the simple paneled style of earlier times when the Colonial Revival came into vogue in the early part of this century.

ETHNIC VARIATIONS MAY OFFER ADDITIONAL CLUES

Knowing about a variety of ethnic variations in fireplaces used during the 1600 and 1700s may help you better date your own fireplace.

DUTCH — the Dutch fireplace was found on the end wall. It featured a hood that was 5 ½ feet from the floor.

FINS AND SWEDES — When the Swedes and Finns settled in Delaware they built one and two-room log homes featuring a corner fireplace made of stone.

GERMAN — The German immigrants of the 18th century built a large off center chimney to accommodate a large kitchen.

HOW TALL IS YOUR HOUSE?

The number of stories (and even its rooms) in your house can be used as a guide to its true age. Here's a look at the most common styles during specific building periods:

PRE REVOLUTION: 1½ stories, often with one main room downstairs and a loft bedroom(s) above).
1790s: 2½ stories
1820s: 3 stories (most common in urban areas)
1840s: 3 stories with mansard roof

CHAPTER TEN:
Your House's Hardware

- NAILS -

It's hard to believe that something as basic as a nail could give away your house's age — but it can! Nails have gone through quite an evolution since the first tree nails (wooden pegs), were used. Getting to know what types of nails were used during particular eras can help you better pinpoint the time span in which your house was built.

HANDMADE WROUGHT IRON NAILS were generally used between 1600-1800. Wrought iron nails are easy to spot. Hand forged by a blacksmith, they vary greatly in style and shape. Their shanks were usually square or rectangular in shape and featured a four-sided taper.

CUT NAILS were first introduced in the latter part of the 1700s, but didn't become common until the 1820s. The early 1700s versions are easy to spot since they had no heads.

By the 1800s two classes of cut nails emerged. The first, (circa 1800-1824), featured a handmade head on a narrow neck, while the second (circa 1825 and beyond), was made by a machine, featuring a flat head which was often stamped with the manufacturer's name on it.

Don't be surprised to find variety in even the machine made nails of the 19th century. The 1825 style was thin and lopsided, replaced a few years later by a thick squared-headed version.

WIRE NAILS were introduced in the latter part of the century. They are categorized by their smaller size and round shafts. Although used as early as the 1820s for finishing work, wire nails didn't become common in general construction until the 1890s.

- HINGES -

Although rare, sometimes homeowners are lucky enough to stumble across a few old hinges in the interior doors of their home that appear to be original. This is often the case in seldom used areas like attics and closets.

How can you tell how old they are? First, check and see what they are made of. Hinges made before the Revolutionary War were always hand-forged from iron. The three most common types are:

CLUE ...

Found a hinge on a door that you think may be original to your house? Check for paint on the surface underneath to make sure. If it's not painted, the odds are the hardware is original.

THE STRAP HINGE, otherwise known as the hook & eye hinge, it resembles a long strap. Bolted against the door, it turns on a hook.

THE H-SHAPED HINGE, resembles the letter H. It is fastened to the door by nails or screws.

THE BUTT HINGE, was first used in the late 1700s. It is small in size and shaped much like a book. Made of cast iron, the butt hinge is less visible than earlier versions, since it fits into the joint at the point where the door and jam meet. The best method of dating a butt hinge is by looking at its pins. From 1800-1830 they featured fixed pins; from 1830-1850 the butts were loose; and after 1850 the hinge itself was usually stamped with the manufacturer's name.

- LATCHES -

Like other door hardware, latches too can be dated. Early thumb-latches were made by blacksmiths from five major pieces: the hand grasp, the lift, the lever, the bar, and the catch. Although there are many individual varieties of latches, the two main styles are the Suffolk and the Norfolk latches.

CLUE...

Where can you find original nails used to build your house? Check the garret floors.

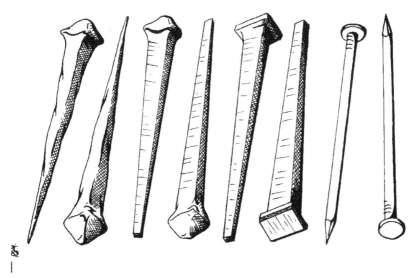

THE EVOLUTION OF NAILS

(from left): #1 & #2: hand wrought nails 1600-1800; #3 & #4: Cut nails (hand headed) 1700-1820; #5 & #6: Cut nails (machine headed) 1700-1850; #7: Wire nails 1820-1900; #8: Wire nails 1900-present.

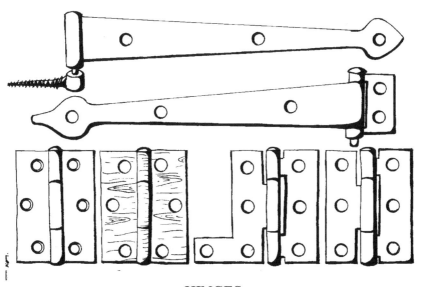

HINGES:

(top): Strap hinge; (from bottom left): case iron butt hinge, wooden butt hinge, HL hinge, H hinge

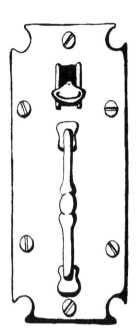

LATCHES (left): Suffolk Latch; (right): Norfolk Latch

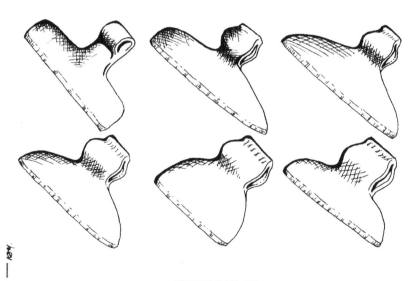

THE BROAD AX
(top left): #1: 1600-1800s; #2: 1700-1800s; #3: 1750-1800
(bottom left): #1: 1750-1800; #2: 1750-1800; #3: 1850-1900

The Suffolk Latch was used from the late 1600s to around 1825, with its popularity hitting its peak in the 18th century. The Suffolk latch is best categorized by its lack of a back plate.

The Norfolk latch was most often used from 1820-1850. It featured a stamped back plate with engraved decorations in the top and bottom. Many featured cast or wrought-iron handles.

- WOOD SCREWS -

Pointed wood screws (like the ones we have today), were not used until after the mid 1800s. Therefore, if you are lucky enough to uncover original wood screws anywhere in your house, check to see if they have blunt or pointed ends. If they are blunt, it is safe to assume that they predate the 1846 version.

PITFALL ...
Finding just a few old nails may not accurately date your house. Nails were often taken from older buildings and recycled in newer ones.

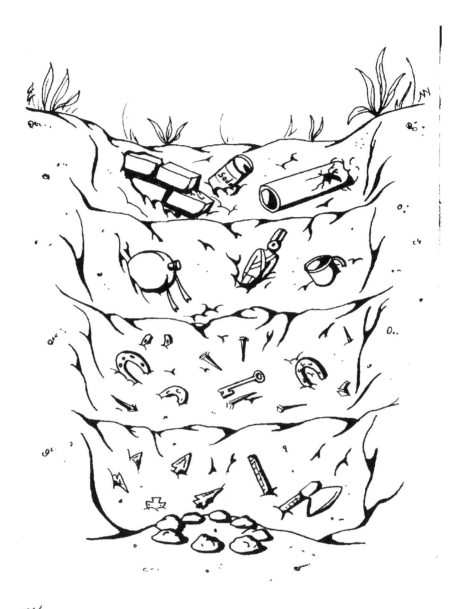

AN ARCHEOLOGICAL DIG

Here are just a sampling of the items you may find from different eras while digging in your backyard:

Bottom layer: 1600-1700, arrow heads, circle of rocks, broken broad ax

Second layer: 1701-1800, horseshoes, iron keys, nails

Third layer: 1801-1900, toy soldier, tin cup, canteen

Top layer: 1900-present, brick foundation, water pipe, soda can

CHAPTER ELEVEN:
Digging Deeper

You can learn a lot about your house (and its former inhabitants), simply by digging around in your backyard.

People always leave behind clues of where they've lived — glass, pottery, broken tools, toys. Your house and grounds are no exception. Everyday items like these can help you discover things you wouldn't have been able to find out any other way. Something as basic as leftover food bones dug up from a trash site can tell you what kinds of food the people who've lived in your house ate on a regular basis, which may tell you about livestock raised on the property.

While this type of information won't date your house per se, it will give you a fascinating overall look at the lives of the people who've lived there. Who knows, you may be lucky enough to uncover datable artifacts such as bottles, early tools, coins or even fashion accessories that can help to pinpoint your house's true age. But be careful, finding a whiskey bottle with a 1780 date inscribed on it doesn't mean your house was standing on the site when that bottle was thrown into the trash. There may have been another house there, or the bottle could have been discarded nonchalantly along a dirt road. As always, take the archeology evidence you uncover and compare the facts you've already learned to create a time line for your house.

Archeology — **digging to learn more about the people who've lived in the past**

- GETTING STARTED -

Excavating your backyard doesn't mean taking a shovel and digging in. The best places to begin any type of archeological dig (even a modest one such as you're about to embark on), is where the artifacts will likely be. In this case you'll want to look for dry wells, cisterns, outhouses, and trash sites. Cisterns, outhouses and wells are often easy to locate. Look for small buildings that may be covering them. Check those old deeds and documents — they may also show their placement. Trash sites may be harder to find since they have more than likely been covered over many times by

Cisterns — **used to catch and store water for household chores**

topsoil. Keep in mind, however, that most trash sites were located in the backs of houses near the kitchen, often located by a stone wall. Another good place to check is beneath any porches, crawl spaces beneath the house and old foundations.

Once you've found a place to begin, you'll need to gather these basic tools:

A Trowel — for scraping away subsoil
A Dust Pan — for removing excavated soil
Graph Paper — for making map/dig sites
A Sturdy Bucket — to hold and carry soil
A Paintbrush — for brushing soil off items
A Ruler — to measure ground depth
A Colander — for sifting small items from the soil
A Camera — for recording item placement in the ground

Digging a site is a lot like reading a book one page at a time. The ground beneath your feet is layered (much like the pages in a book). About every one hundred years, 8-12 inches of topsoil builds up on top of the soil already there, creating datable layers (see the diagram at the beginning of the chapter). These layers may offer valuable clues about specific periods in time. Therefore, the deeper you dig, the further back in time you'll travel. For instance, to reach discarded items from the 1800s, you'll need to dig about 2 feet into the ground.

If this sounds difficult, don't worry. Just remember to dig slowly and be careful. To better preserve the site you may want to employ the scrape method used by professional archeologists. Instead of digging (which can harm fragile artifacts), archeologists actually scrape away levels of dirt. It's more tedious than digging, but much less risky. Once scraped off, loose dirt is then taken from the site and sifted through a wire mesh screen (in this case a simple kitchen colander should work nicely), so that small items such as coins, buttons and pieces of broken pottery aren't accidentally lost in the dirt.

Don't get discouraged if you can't find anything right away. Any type of archeological dig takes time and patience. There may be a lot of interesting things buried in your yard, you just haven't uncovered them yet.

The most important part of any archeological dig is not the actual digging, but the record-keeping. Whenever you uncover anything, (a toy, bottle, or even a broken tool), measure the depth of the soil. This will help you determine the time period in which the item was discarded. You may even want to draw a diagram of the site on graph paper to help you better visualize its location later. Whatever you do, don't get so caught up in the excitement of finally finding something that you rush on and keep digging. Here's where your patience pays off. By taking the time to record your find accurately, you'll be able to better date the dig later.

Now's the time to snap a few pictures, carefully wash the item, number it and tag it so you don't forget any pertinent information that you may need.

The things you uncover will probably be basic household items. However, if, at any time, you believe you stumble across an artifact that may hold special historic significance to either your town, county, state or even federal history, it's best to call in experts to finish the job you've already started. Local archeological experts can be found through your local historical preservation office, historical society, college campus or state government.

WHAT KINDS OF THINGS CAN I EXPECT TO FIND IN MY BACKYARD?

Every household dig is different. Some uncover interesting artifacts such as pieces of old diaries and ledgers, while others only uncover a multitude of useless and broken junk. Usually, however, at least a few worthwhile items are found, making it worth the digger's time and trouble.

On the average these are the types of items you may find on your own property:

POTTERY — even if you can't find a date inscribed on it, don't despair. Sometimes the decoration and even the shape of a piece of pottery can help you date it.

GLASS — types and styles can tell you a lot, but look carefully, some bottles even have small dates on them.

FOOD REMNANTS — it may sound disgusting, but leftover chicken bones may signal a henhouse on the premises, while a variety of wild game bones would signify that most of the household meat came from hunting in nearby woods.

TOYS — often lost and discarded, toys are a great way to date a property. Marbles, doll parts, pottery tea sets, bone dominoes and instruments can all be easily dated.

TOOLS — broken tools were often thrown in trash sites. Since tools have evolved over the years, discarded ones are an excellent dating source.

SECTION III:

THE NEXT STEP

SECTION III:
Introduction

It wasn't so long ago that old houses were torn down to make way for newer, more modern ones. Not anymore. In recent years, people have begun to see the value in preserving our past, so that we can better appreciate our future.

Until now, your house history search required digging around for information, whether in an old dusty basement archive or your backyard. Now it's time to think about the next step. Section III will help you make such important decisions as:

* whether to restore or renovate your old house
* how to record your house's history
* what it means to put your house on a historic register, and how to do it.

CHAPTER TWELVE:
Renovation or Restoration?

The fact is, you are an old house lover. If you weren't, you wouldn't have taken the time and energy to even begin such a comprehensive genealogical search of your home. The problem with old house lovers is that they love the history of their old houses so much, they often are tempted to join the ranks of amateur preservationists and turn their home into nothing more than a lived -in museum.

Before you start running wild with visions of returning your house to its original splendor, wait! Living in a restored 1780s farmhouse may sound romantic, but is it? Really? In its truest sense, restoration involves returning a building to its exact appearance during a chosen period in history. Not only is this approach expensive, it's simply impractical if you plan to continue living there. After all, restoring that 18th century farmhouse would mean foregoing such modern conveniences as a stove and refrigerator and returning to fireplace cooking and icehouse cooling. Not to mention ripping out your bathroom (gasp!) And digging yourself a brand new outhouse in the backyard (ugh!).

Now that I've grabbed your attention and completely thwarted all of your dreams of a major restoration project, you may be wondering just how you can bring alive the best of your house's past while still enjoying life in the future. Thankfully, there are a few options to consider:

PRESERVATION is one way to accomplish your goal. Still rather expensive, this method allows the homeowner to restore, repair and maintain the building in the state in which it survived. Simply put, preservation allows you to "restore" sections of your home to its practical past without forgoing the conveniences you're used to. For instance, a preservationist might attack the bathroom in a Victorian Home by remodeling it to appear older by using turn of the century fixtures, lighting, flooring and a claw foot tub. These types of touches will give the room the Victorian flair, while still allowing you to enjoy modern day soaks.

REHABILITATION is the most common approach used by private old house owners. Rehabilitating an older building requires making the home useful again while retaining its original character-defining features, such as exterior gingerbread, interior staircases, fireplaces, etc. Rehabilitation allows the homeowner to change or add whatever they see fit in the house, as long as a few major features are kept to help the house retain its historical character to a certain degree.

RENOVATION is similar to rehabilitation, but introduces even more new material to the building.

REMODELING on the other hand, generally involves changing almost everything about the house, including its style. Old details are stripped away and replaced with more modern ones. A remodeled old house virtually becomes a new house, leaving behind little (if any) of the elements that gave it its historic flavor.

Of course, these too are only guidelines. Some homeowners opt to mix and match these options. For instance, if a modern kitchen is important to you, you may opt to remodel the kitchen, but actually restore the sitting room. The decisions are ultimately up to you and must fit your lifestyle, interests and budget. To help you decide how best to preserve the flavor of your older home, ask yourself these questions:

IS MY HOUSE WORTH THE TIME AND EXPENSE A MAJOR PROJECT WILL COST? Of course you love your house, and you are enthralled with all the new things you've recently learned about its past. But is that enough to justify spending thousands of dollars (and even more hours) preserving, restoring or renovating it one room at a time? Before beginning any major project, consider your house's age, its condition, current value, future value, its historic significance to the community (if any) and its architectural interest.

DO I HAVE THE TIME TO DEVOTE TO THIS PROJECT? No project is worse than an unfinished project. Even if you can afford to hire others to do the actual work on your house, you'll still need a large chunk of time to scour area antique stores, fixture shops and catalogues looking for antique and reproduction items to make your historic house project as accurate as possible.

DO I HAVE THE MONEY REQUIRED TO MAKE MY HOME AN HISTORIC HOUSE? Whether you want to simply restore a room or the entire house (inside and out), it's going to take money — and lots of it. Any remodeling project runs into unexpected costs. Even more so in an old home. Here's a good rule of thumb: whatever you think a specific project is going to cost, double or even triple that amount and you'll be closer to the actual cost.

Think you still want to go ahead with your special preservation project? Don't start everything at once. Begin with a single room, or, better yet, a single element like the walls, floors or fixtures, and then move on from there. If a tight budget is keeping you from turning your 19th century home into a Victorian wonder consider a few smaller scale but eye catching projects such as :

* sprucing up those worn out floors. Nothing adds more sparkle to a home than sanding and staining tired hardwood floors. Although a fairly cheap project, keep in mind it's time consuming and messy!

* Bring your staircase back to life. The staircase used to be the center point of the entire home. Take the time to restore it to its original splendor and you won't be disappointed.

* Add old fashioned lighting fixtures. Such a simple (and relatively inexpensive) thing to do, yet it can add so much historic flavor to an older home

* Repaint. The exterior of a house says a lot about it and the people who live in it. Don't have the time or money to work on the inside? Then concentrate on making your house look its age by giving it a fresh coat of historically accurate paint.

* Small touches do count. Remember, no matter what your tastes, small touches such as switch plates, pictures, cabinet hardware, etc. all can add that touch of old-time flavor that your house has been

missing. Use your research to give your house that special decorating touch. Found old pictures while digging through old historical society papers? Ask if you can get copies. Then mat and frame them for hanging in a prominent spot in your foyer or living room. Uncovered some interesting tidbits while excavation and old well? Dust them off and simply put them in a small cabinet for others to enjoy. Take the time to figure out what makes your house special, then use it to show others what a great old house you really do have.

CHAPTER THIRTEEN:
Writing Your House's Story

You've finished your research. Now what do you do with the information you've gathered? It's time to gather all your notes and compile them into a readable format.

Before setting pen to paper though, you'll first want to think about the kind of biography you want to write. A time line is relatively easy to do. It's a chronological list of the facts pertaining to your house (when it was built, sold, remodeled, etc.), with short narratives explaining the most important entries. For example, a time line might look something like this:

JAN 5, 1862 — First Deed Recorded

1902 — Daughter Inherits House

1908 — Building Permits Indicate Major Renovations

to Kitchen

Another option is the detailed narrative that highlights all of the important events in your house's history including facts on the families who've lived there, how the house was decorated, a rundown of technological advances it has undergone, and more. Depending on the house's age and history, this can be done in a brief 10-50 page report or a full length manuscript.

Whether you choose to write a brief historical perspective or a complete book, remember, your job as a house historian is to not only gather good facts, but to interpret them in a way that show readers your house's true history.

Where should you begin? Start with a thorough review of your notes. Next, decide on your focus. Do you want to cover specific building eras and the architectural changes your house underwent during those times, or would you rather delve into the day to day lives of your house's past occupants?

No matter what your focus, every house biography should include:

* a description of the geographic location in relation to the community
* a chronological sequence of events pertaining to the property
* a detailed description of the architectural & technological changes the house has undergone

How deep you want to delve into these and other aspects of the property is completely up to you. The type of information you include in the biography will depend a great deal on who your target audience is. If you're writing it primarily for yourself and the house's future owners, a time line may be sufficient. If, however, you intend to use your research to apply for local, state or federal historic status (more on this in the next chapter), you'll need to include detailed material that shows the property's historic significance.

- HOW TO WRITE A HOUSE'S BIOGRAPHY -

What a challenge it is to write a biography that not only expresses your house's fascinating past, but does it in a way that will excite the reader! How can you accomplish such a grand goal? First, don't just list the cold hard facts. Make your house's past come alive. Tell its story. Use lots of details. Help your reader visualize what the house looked like in 1842 or 1963. What style wallpaper adorned the walls? Where was the coat closet? Were there two bedrooms, three, four? How about the yard? Was there an outhouse? Barn? Chicken coop? Simple details like these will help turn those ho-hum facts into a real page turner.

Whatever you do, don't try to impress the reader with your writing ability. Use simple words and phrases. People don't want to dig through endless pages of huge words and hard-to-read sentences. They want reader-friendly material that they can enjoy.

- PUTTING IT ALL TOGETHER -

Thanks to today's high tech computer programs and inexpensive printing options, just about anyone can write and publish a good quality (and reasonably priced) book. Whether you're putting together a 20-page booklet or a perfect-bound edition, it can be done more cheaply and easily than ever before.

The first thing you need to decide is its size. Will it be a standard size, oversize, or a small pocket-sized volume? How many pages will it have? 100? 200? 300?

Answering these two basic questions will tell you whether you need a full-service printer or a local quick press copy shop. The major rule of thumb is this: if you want less than 200 copies, let the copy shop do it. Printers work with volume, especially on such labor intensive projects. While you may be able to find a printer that will do such a short run, you'll pay handsomely for it.

If you're worried that your local quick press can't do as professional a job as a printer, don't! Today's copy shops are equipped to handle a variety of book sizes, covers and paper styles. A variety of binding options are also available including glue, staples, spiral, among others.

Next, you'll want to decide how many (and what kind of) illustrations your book will include, since this will affect the final price more than anything else. Although more expensive, this type of book begs for loads of pictures to help give the text more meaning.

Finally, you'll need to consider layout. In general, reference books of this kind should include the following:

Title Page
Preface
Table of Contents
Chapters
Appendix
Bibliography
Index

Now that you know the basics, it's time to get writing. Oh, and don't forget to have fun!

HIRING A PROFESSIONAL BIOGRAPHER

At this point you may be wondering, "should I hire a professional biographer?" For some the answer will be a resounding "yes." For others, "no."

Hiring a professional may be a good idea if:

1. You're Rich
2. You Hate To Write
3. You're Planning To Sell Your Book For Profit
4. You Want To Apply For Federal Historic Status

Even if the above is true, that doesn't mean that you can't do a great job yourself. After all, no one knows your house — and its history — better than you. And no one can get more excited about the project than you.

That said, if you still feel that only a professional writer can do the job, then by all means go for it. Keep in mind that it can be costly though. Fees for this type of project run from $1,000- $20,000 or more, depending on the skill and experience of the writer.

The hardest part is locating a competent writer. Ask around. Call your local college or university. They may have a professor on staff who specializes in this type of writing. Check with your local historical society and museums. They too may be able to recommend someone.

Place a help wanted ad in the local newspaper, or contact one of the writers' organizations listed in the appendix.

And never hire the first (or cheapest) writer who comes along without carefully checking references, reviewing clips (samples of their work) and getting a formal bid for the project. After all, this is the culmination of all your hard work, you want to make sure you choose the best person for the job.

CHAPTER 14:
Giving Your House Historic Significance

You've done it! Your research is complete. Now what? For some, the final step to their house history project is giving their home historical status by placing it in one or more registers designed to identify and promote public awareness of historically significant buildings.

In its simplest term, an historic register is an inventory of historic properties in a certain town, district, county, state or nation. There are literally thousands of different registers throughout the nation. Some, such as local or neighborhood registers, are fairly easy to get on. Others, like the National Register of Historic Places require a complex application process that can take years of research and documentation to complete. So, before digging into those applications, you'll want to carefully consider the reason(s) why you are interested in listing your home on one of these registers.

If it's recognition that you're after, then a town or county register will probably fill your need. Local registers are a great way for people to show the community the historic significance of their home, without devoting a lot of time and money to the project. Individual municipality and county register recipients are usually allowed to display an impressive plaque on their home's exterior to showcase their house's unique significance to the community.

If, on the other hand, you want to use the registration process to obtain special tax credits, grants or other preservation assistance for your home, a state or federal listing is probably what you're after. One note of caution here: these types of registers are difficult and time consuming to get on. It can also be expensive, since many people find it difficult to complete the in-depth applications themselves and must hire experts to do it for them — all with no guarantee of a final listing.

No matter which type of historic register you are interested in applying for, there are a few basic requirements you'll need to fulfill.

Even the most basic local register will require the applicant to prove his/her property's significance, whether through its architecture, age, previous ownership, prior use, etc. The more impressive the register, the harder it will be to prove. Simply owning a 100-year-old house isn't going to be enough to get you further than your town register, no matter how old or beautiful your home. You'll need to find a link between your house's past and the county, state or nation's history. That said, let's move on to the actual application processes.

To find out if your township or borough has its own historic register, call the municipal building or local historic society. They should be able to provide you with a list of criteria and an application. The application for local registers is usually easy (less than 10 pages), to complete. No matter how simple the application, don't be sloppy in giving facts. If you decide to go on with the registration process in the future, you'll need to use all previous applications to help prove what you say in the next one.

County Registers are generally a little more in-depth, yet still pretty simple, since the only thing the applicant must prove is a local link between their house and the county's history.

Move onto the state application process and you've now entered the big leagues. Suddenly, the criteria increase, as does the paper-work. Now it's time to get down to work. Befriend your State Historic Preservation Officer (SHOP). He or she is your best ally in obtaining both the state and federal recognition your house deserves. They hold important roles in the nomination process, since they are the ones who will review your documentation and actually nominate the property to the review board. In most states, the SHOP is the one who fights for the listing and actually makes the final decision whether or not to send the application on to the National Register board.

Besides, SHOPs are experts in historic documentation research. They understand the process, and aren't intimidated by it. When a question arises, ask! It's not only their job to help — most love the challenge.

While most state registers are infinitely easier to get on than the federal one, don't be complacent. Listing any house on a state historic register is difficult. Private homes are the hardest. As the process continues, you'll find yourself vying for space next to actual "landmarks," so you had better be ready and able to prove why your house deserves to be on it in the first place.

There are three main concepts used to determine whether a property qualifies for a listing on both the state and the national listing: historic significance, historical integrity and historical context. Now, let's discuss each briefly:

HISTORICAL SIGNIFICANCE is the importance of a property in relation to the history, architecture, archeology, engineering or culture of the community, state or nation. To determine a house's historic significance you must consider:
- its association with specific historic events or activities
- its association with important persons
- its distinctive physical characteristics (design, structure, form)
- its potential yield of important information

HISTORICAL CONTEXT links historic properties to important historic trends using theme, place and time. Historic context allows the property (and its historic significance) to be seen in relation to the trends and patterns of the entire community, and the part it played in it. For instance, themes may relate to the historic development of a community such as commercial or industrial activities, the rise of an architectural movement, the work of a master architect, specific events, or a pattern of physical development that influenced the character of a place.

HISTORICAL INTEGRITY allows the property to keep a sense of its past through surviving physical characteristics. Historic integrity is a composite of these seven qualities:
- location
- design
- setting
- materials
- workmanship

- feeling
- association

Assuming that you feel that your house fits these three main components, it's now time to start the actual registration process. The National Register of Historic Places' application has twelve sections:
- name of property
- location
- state/federal agency certification
- national park service certification
- classification
- function or use
- description
- statement of significance
- major bibliographical references
- geographical data
- form prepared by
- additional documentation

Here's a brief rundown of the requirements of each of these sections.
NAME OF PROPERTY. Here you'll need to enter an historic name for your property. Choose one that best reflects the historic importance of your home, or one that was commonly used for the property during a specific time during its history (ex: Doc Browne's Office; Wilson Farm, etc).
LOCATION. A simple requirement. Here, you simply enter the street and number where your house is located.
STATE/FEDERAL AGENCY CERTIFICATION. This your SHOP will complete.
NATIONAL PARK SERVICE CERTIFICATION. The National Park Service completes this section
CLASSIFICATION. Here you'll need to mark whether your home is privately or publicly owned, and by whom.
FUNCTION OR USE. Here your job starts to get a bit tougher. In this section, you will be required to chronicle the functions your property has served during specific periods in its history.

DESCRIPTION. This is a very important section for properties with architectural importance. Using a specially-designed list, the applicant must describe the property's architectural styles and stylistic influences relating to a general period of time.

STATEMENT OF SIGNIFICANCE. For this section, the applicant must choose the area of significance in which the property best fits. Study the criteria listed in the application before choosing. When writing your final statement of significance be sure that you've clearly stated the reasons why the property meets the National Register criteria, then back up your reasoning with a chronological history of the property. Be specific about references to history and geography. Give dates and proper names of owners, builders, architects, .whenever possible. Finally, include descriptive historical information about the area where the property is located.

MAJOR BIBLIOGRAPHICAL REFERENCES are your list of sources (both primary and secondary), which you used when researching your property. These include books, journals, articles, advertisements, documents, surveys, interviews, photographs, census data, etc. In short, any material used to document facts about your house and its history. Use a standard bibliographical style when completing this section.

GEOGRAPHICAL DATA defines the location and extent of the property being nominated. It also explains why the boundaries were selected. Review the guidelines included in your application packet carefully before making a selection.

FORM PREPARED BY identifies the person who prepared the document and his/her affiliation to the property. Since some homeowners opt to pay a professional to prepare state and federal register documents, this section enables the National Park Service to save time when they have questions, by contacting the person who actually completed the application

ADDITIONAL DOCUMENTATION may include maps, photographs, notarized letters, comments from government officials, etc. Submitting any type of additional documents with the federal application has its own individual requirements. Never submit any additional information without first checking these guidelines.

Once you've filled out the appropriate paperwork to place your home on any historic register, the final step is waiting. Good Luck!

Congratulations, your house history is complete! It was a long, tough journey, but hopefully, you've walked away from your search with a deeper understanding and appreciation of the role your house played in your community's (or even the nation's) history. Once you've dug deep into your house's past, one thing is certain, you'll never walk through your house and look at its rooms quite the same way again.

FIND OUT MORE ABOUT THE NATIONAL REGISTER OF HISTORIC PLACES

The National Register's web site gives all of the requirements/criteria for the applying for federal historic status. Download everything you need from the application itself, to complete instructions and examples, as well as a history of the Register.

Visit the site at: http://www.cr.nps.gov

APPENDIX A:
State Historic Preservation Offices

ALABAMA
Mr. F. Lawrence Oaks
State Historic preservation Officer & Executive Director, Alabama
Historic Commission
468 South Perry Street
Montgomery, Alabama, 36130—0900
(334) 242—3184
lawereOaks @ aol.com

ALASKA
Ms. Judith E. Bittner
Chief, History & Archeology Department of Natural Resources
Division of Parks and Outdoor Recreation
3601 C. Street, Suite 1278
Anchorage, Alaska 99503—5921
(907) 269—8715

ARIZONA
Mr. James Garrison
State Historic Preservation Officer
Office of Historic Preservation
Arizona State Parks
1300 W. Washington
Phoenix, Arizona 85007
(602) 542—4009

ARKANSAS
Mrs. Cathryn H. Slater
Director, Arkansas Historic Preservation Program
1500 Tower Building
323 Center Street

Little Rock, Arkansas 72201
(501) 324—9880
info @dah.state.ar.us

CALIFORNIA
Ms. Cherilyn Widell
State Historic Preservation Officer
Office of Historic Preservation
Department of Parks & Recreation
P.O. Box 942896
Sacramento, California 94296—0001
(916) 653—6624

COLORADO
Mr. James E. Hartmann
State Historic Preservation Officer and President, Colorado Historical Society
Colorado History Museum
1300 Broadway
Denver, Colorado 80203—2137
(303) 866—3355

CONNECTICUT
Mr. John W. Shannahan
State Historic Preservation Officer and Director, Connecticut Historical Commission
59 South Prospect Street
Hartford, Connecticut 06106
(203) 566—3005

DELAWARE
Mr. Daniel R. Griffith
Director, Division of Historical & Cultural Affairs
Hall of Records
P.O. Box 1401
Dover, Delaware 19901
(302) 739—5313

DISTRICT OF COLUMBIA
Mr. Wilbert J. Parker
State Historic Preservation Officer
Department of Consumer & Regulatory Affairs
614 H. Street, NW   Suite 1120
Washington, D.C. 20001
(202) 727—7120

FLORIDA
R.A. Gray Building
500 South Bronough Street
Tallahassee, Florida 32399—0250
(850) 488—1480

GEORGIA
Mr. Mark R. Edwards
Director, Historic Preservation Division
Department of Natural Resources
500 The Healey Building
57 Forsyth Street, NW
Atlanta, Georgia 30303
(404) 656—2840

HAWAII
Mr. Michael D. Wilson
State Historic Preservation Officer
Department of Land & Natural Resources
1151 Punchbowl Street
Honolulu, Hawaii 96813
(808) 548—6550

IDAHO
Dr. Robert M.Yohe, III
Interim State Historic Preservation Officer
210 Main Street
Boise, Idaho 83702
(208) 334—3890

ILLINOIS
Mr. William L. Wheeler
Associate Director, Illinois Historic Preservation Agency
Preservation Services Division
One Old State Capitol Plaza
Springfield, Illinois 62701
(217) 785—9045
(St. Address: 500 E.Madison)

INDIANA
Mr. Larry D. Macklin
State Historic Preservation Officer & Director, Department of Natural
Resources
402 West washington Street, Room W 274
Indianapolis, Indiana 46204
(317) 232—4020
dhpa—at—dnrlan @ima.isd.state.in.us

IOWA
Mr. Tom Morain
Administrator and SHOP
State Historical Society of Iowa
600 East Locust Street
Des Moines, Iowa 50319—0209
(515) 281—8837

KANSAS
Mr. Ramon S. Powers
Executive Director, Kansas State Historical Society
Cultural Resources Division
6425 Southwest 6th Avenue
Topeka, Kansas 66615—1099
(913) 272—8681 ext. 205

KENTUCKY
Mr. David Morgan
State Historic Preservation officer & Director, Kentucky heritage
Council
300 Washington Street
Frankfort, Kentucky 40601
(502) 564—7005
dmorgan @mail.state.ky.us

LOUISIANA
Mrs. Gerri J. Hobdy
Assistant Secretary, Office of Cultural Development
P.O. Box 44247
Baton Rouge, Louisiana 70804
(504) 342—8200

MAINE
Mr. Earle G. Shettleworth, Jr.
Director, Maine Historic Preservation Commission
55 Capital Street
Station 65
Augusta, Maine 04333—0065
(207) 287—2132
Sheshet @state.me.us

MARYLAND
Mr. J. Rodney Little
Executive Director, Historical and Cultural Programs
Department of Housing & Community Development
Peoples resource Center
100 Community Place
Crownsville, Maryland 21032—2023
(410) 514—7600
mdshpo @ari.met

MASSACHUSETTS
Mrs. Judith B. McDonough
State Historic Preservation Officer & Executive Director, Massachusetts Historical Commission
Massachusetts Archives Facility
220 Morrissey Boulevard
Boston, Massachusetts 02125
(617) 727—8570
JmcDonough @mhc.sec.state.ma.us

MICHIGAN
Mr. Brian Conway
State Historic Preservation Office
Michigan State Historic Preservation Office
Michigan Historical Center
717 W. Allegan
Lansing, Michigan 48918
(517) 373—0511
cecilM @sosmail.state.mi.us

MINNESOTA
Dr. Nina M. Archibal
Director, Minnesota Historical Society, State Historic Preservation Office
345 Kellogg Boulevard West
St. Paul, Minnesota 55102
(612) 296—2747

MISSISSIPPI
Mr. Elbert Hilliard
Director, State of Mississippi Department of Archives & History
P.O.Box 571
Jackson, Mississippi 39205
(601) 359—6850
msshpo @mdah.ms.us

MISSOURI
Mr. Stephan Mahfood
Director, Department of Natural Resources
P.O. Box 176
Jefferson City, Missouri 65102
(314) 751—4732

MONTANA
Mr. Paul Putz
State Historic Preservation Officer, Montana Historical Society
1410 8th Avenue
P.O. Box 201202
Helena, Montana 59602—1202
(406) 444—7715

NEBRASKA
Mr. Lawrence J. Sommer
Director, Nebraska State Historical Society
1500 R. Street
P.O. Box 82554
Lincoln, Nebraska 68501
(402) 471—4787

NEVADA
Mr. Ronald M. James
State Historic Preservation Officer, Department of Museums, Library
& Arts
100 S. Stewart Street
Capital Complex
Carson City, Nevada 89710
(702) 687—6360
rmjames @lahontan.clan.lib.nv.us

NEW HAMPSHIRE
Mrs. Nancy Muller
Director, Division of Historical Resources
P.O. Box 2043
Concord, New Hampshire 03302—2043
(603) 271—6435

NEW JERSEY
Mr. Robert C. Shinn, Jr.
Commissioner, Department of Environmental Protection
CN—402, 401 East State Street
Trenton, New Jersey 08625
(609) 292—2885

NEW MEXICO
Dr. Lynne Sebastian
Director, State Historic Preservation Division, office of Cultural
Affairs
Villa Rivera Building, 3rd floor
228 East Palace Avenue
Santa Fe, New Mexico 87503
(505) 827—6320

NEW YORK
Mrs. Bernadette Castro
Commissioner, Office of Parks, Recreation & Historic Preservation
Empire State Plaza
Agency Building 1, 20th floor
Albany, New York 12238
(518) 474—0443

NORTH CAROLINA
Dr. Jeffrey J. Crow
Director, Department of Cultural Resources, Division of Archives &
History
109 East Jones Street
Raleigh, North Carolina 27601—2807

NORTH DAKOTA
Mr. James E. Sperry
Superintendent, State Historical Society of North Dakota
ND heritage Center
612 east Boulevard Avenue
Bismarck, North Dakota 58505
(701) 328—2672
jsperry @ranch.state.nd.us

OHIO
Dr. Amos J. Loveday, Jr.
State Historic Preservation Officer
Historic Preservation Division
Ohio Historical Society
567 E. Hudson Street
Columbus, Ohio 43211—1030
(614) 297—2470

OKLAHOMA
Mr. J. Blake Wade
Executive Director, Oklahoma Historical Society & Historic
Preservation Officer
Wiley Post Historical Building
2100 N. Lincoln Boulevard
Oklahoma City, Oklahoma 73105
(405) 521—6249

OREGON
Mr. Robert L. Meinen
Director, State Parks & Recreation Department
1115 Commercial Street NE
Salem, Oregon 97310—1001
(503) 378—5019
James.m.hamrick @state.or.us

PENNSYLVANIA
Dr. Brent D. Glass
State Historic Preservation Officer, Pennsylvania Historical &
Museum Commission
P.O. Box 1026
Harrisburg, Pennsylvania 17108—1026
(717) 787—2891

RHODE ISLAND
Mr. Frederick C. Williamson
State Historic Preservation Officer, Historic Preservation Commission
Old State House
150 Benefit Street
Providence, Rhode Island 02903
(401) 222—2678

SOUTH CAROLINA
Dr. Rodger E. Stroup
Director, Department of Archives and History
831 Parklane Road
Columbia, South Carolina 29223—4905
(803) 734—8592

SOUTH DAKOTA
Mr. Jay D. Vogt
Acting State Historic Preservation Officer, State Historical Society
Historic Preservation
900 Governors Drive
Pierre, South Dakota 57501—2217
(605) 773—3458
jayv @chc.state.sd.us

TENNESSEE
Mr. Ollie Keller

Deputy Commissioner, Department of Environment & Conservation
& Historic Preservation
2941 Labanon Road
Nashville, Tennessee 37243—0435
(615) 532—0105

TEXAS
Mr. Curtis Tunnell
Executive Director, Texas Historical Commission
P.O. Box 12276, Capital Station
Austin, Texas 78711
(512) 463—6100
www.thc.state.tx.us

UTAH
Mr. Max J. Evans
State Historic Preservation Officer & Director, Utah State Historical
Society
300 Rio Grande
Salt Lake City, Utah 84101
(801) 533—3551
cehistry.ushs @email.state.ut.us

VERMONT
Ms. Emily Wadhams
Historic Preservation Officer & Director, Agency of Commerce &
Community Development
Vermont Division of Historic Preservation
National Life Building, Drawer 20
Montpelier, Vermont 05620—0501
(802) 828—3056

VIRGINIA
Mr. H. Alexander Wise, Jr.
Director, Department of Historic Resources
2801 Kensington Avenue

Richmond, Virginia 23221
(804) 367—2323

WASHINGTON
Mr. David Hansen
Acting State Historic Preservation Officer
Office of Archeology & Historic Preservation
Washington State Department of Community, Trade & Economic
Development
111 West 21ˢᵗ Avenue, Box 48343SW
Olympia, Washington 98504—8343
(360) 407—0765
davidh @acted.wa.gov

WEST VIRGINIA
Ms. Renay Conlin
Commissioner, Division of Culture & History
Capital Complex
Charleston, West Virginia 25305
(304) 558—0200

WISCONSIN
Dr. George L. Vogt
State Historic Preservation Officer & Director, Historic Preservation
Division
816 State Street
Madison, Wisconsin 53706
(608) 264—6500

WYOMING
Mr. John T. Keck
State Historic Preservation Officer, Department of Commerce
6101 Yellowstone
Cheynenne, Wyoming 82002
(307) 777—7697

APPENDIX B:
Additional Resources

PRESERVATION GROUPS

National Trust For Historic Preservation
Mr. Richard Moe, president
National Trust for Historic Preservation
1785 Massachusetts Avenue, NW
Washington, D.C. 20036
(202) 588—6000

National Conference of State Historic Preservation Officers (Ncshpo)
Mr. Eric Hertfelder, executive director
NCSHPO
Hall of States
444 No. Capitol Street, NW., Suite 332
Washington, D.C. 20001
(202) 624—5465

The Advisory Council on Historic Preservation
Mr. John Fowler, acting Director
The Old Post Office Building
1100 Pennsylvania Avenue NW., Suite 809
Washington, D.C. 20004
(202) 606—8503

Advisory Council on Historic Preservation
Office of Education and Preservation
Mr. Ronald D. Anzalone, director
Old Post Office Building
1100 Pennsylvania Avenue NW., Suite 803
Washington, D.C. 20004
(202) 606—8505

National Institute for the Conservation of Cultural Property
Mr. Lawrence L. Reger, president
3299 K Street NW., Suite 602
Washington, D.C. 20037
(202) 625—1485

National Park Service
Heritage Preservation Services
Ms. Tawana Jackson
1849 C Street NW., Suite NC200
Washington, D.C. 20240
(202) 343—9565

American Association for State and Local History
172 Second Avenue, North, Suite 102
Nashville, TN 37204

Center for Historic Houses
1785 Massachusetts Avenue, NW
Washington, D.C. 20036

National Building Museum
Pension Building
Judiciary Square, NW
Washington, D.C. 20001

Preservation Action
1350 Connecticut Avenue, NW, Suite 400—A
Washington, D.C. 20036
(202) 659—0915

GENEALOGICAL ORGANIZATIONS

Daughters of the American Revolution
1776 D. Street, NW
Washington, D.C. 20006
(202)879—3229

National Genealogical Society Library
4527 17th Street, N.
Arlington, VA 22207
(703) 525—0050

Western Reserve Historical Society
10825 East Boulevard
Cleveland, Ohio 44106
(216) 721—5722

Bureau of Land Management (Dept. Of the Interior)
1849 C Street NW
Washington, D.C. 20204
(202) 343—9435

Automated Records Systems
7450 Boston Blvd.
Springfield, VA 22153—3121
(703) 440—1600

U.S. Census Bureau
1201 E.10th Street
P.O. Box 1545
Jeffersonville, IN 47131
(812) 285—5314

MAGAZINES

Early American Homes
6405 Flank Drive
Harrisburg, Pa. 17112
(717) 657—9552

Old—house Interiors
2 Main Street
Glouchester, MA 01930
(978) 283—3200

Old House Journal
2 Main Street
Glouchecter, MA 01930
(978) 283—3200

Victorian Homes
265 S. Anita Drive, Suite 120
Orange, CA 92868—3310
(714) 939—9991

OTHER USEFUL ADDRESSES

U.S. Copyright Office
Library of Congress
Thomas Jefferson Building
1st—2nd Streets, NW
Washington, D.C. 20540

U.S. Department of the Interior
P.O. Box 25425
Denver, Co. 80225

BIBLIOGRAPHY

Authentic Door Catalogue. Hendricks Woodworking Company. 1998.

Beller, Susan Provost. *Roots for Kids, A Genealogy Guide for Young People.* Betterway Books. 1989.

Bureau of Naval Personnel. *Tools and Their Uses.* 1971.

Comstock, William T. *Turn—of—the—Century House Designs.* Dover Publications. 1994

Comstock, William T. *Victorian Domestic Architectural Plans.* Dover Publications. 1987.

Croom, Emily. *The Genealogist's Companion and Sourcebook.* Betterway Books. 1994.

Crummings, M.F. and Miller, C.C. *Designs for Street Fronts, Suburban Houses, Catalogue.* 1865.

Evers, Christopher. *The Old House Doctor.* Overlook Press. 1986.

Gillon, Edmund V., Jr. *Victorian Houses.* Dover Publications. 1979.

Gudknecht, Edward R. *A Homeowner's Guide to Good Deeds.* 1989.

Hagedorn, Nancy L. and Gaynor, James M. *Tools — Working Wood in 18th Century America.* Colonial Williamsburg Foundation Press. 1993.

Hartley, William G. *The Everything Family Tree Book.* Adams Media Corp. 1998.

Hilowitz, Beverly and Green, Susan Eikov. *Historic Houses of America.* Simon and Schuster Publishing. 1980.

Howard, Hugh. *How Old Is This House?* Noonday Press. 1989.

Light, Sally. *House Histories.* Golden Hill Press. 1989.

McAllester, Virginia & Lee. *A Field Guide To American Houses.* A. Knopf Inc. 1984

McNealy, Terry A. *How To Find The Story of An Old House.* Bucks County Historical Society. 1988.

Moss, Roger W. *Paint in America. The Colors of Historic Buildings.* National Trust for Historic Preservation Press. 1994.

Nylander, Richard C. *Wall Papers for Historic Buildings.* John Wiley & SonsInc. 1992.

Pappliers, John and Chambers, S. Allen and Schwartz, Nancy B. *What Style Is It?* Preservation Press. 1966.

Mercer, Dr. Henry C. *The Dating of Old Houses.* Bucks County Historical Society. 1923.

Morrison, Hugh. *Early American Architecture.* Dover Publications. 1987.

National Park Service Preservation Services. State, Tribal and Local Programs Branch. 1998.

Orme, Alan Dan. *Reviving Old Houses.* Storey Communications. 1989.

Roberts, E.L. *Roberts' Illustrated Millwork Catalogue.* 1903

Samford, Patricia and Ribblett, David. *Archeology For Young Explorers.* Colonial Williamsburg Foundation Press. 1997.

Sears, Roebuck and Co. Home Builders Catalogue. 1910.

Sherwood, Gerald, E. *How To Select and Renovate An Older House.* Dover Publications. 1976.

Shoppell, R.W. *Turn—of—the—Century Houses, Cottages and Villas.* Dover Publications. 1983.

Sloane, Eric. *A Museum of American Tools.* Ballantine Books. 1964.

Smith, A.G. *The American House, Styles of Architecture.* Dover Publications. 1983.

Smith, Elmer L. *Early Lighting, From Tallow to Oil in Early America.* Applied Arts Publishers. 1997.

Sperry, Kip. *Reading Early American Writing.* Genealogical Publishing Company. 1998.

Stephen, George. *Remodeling Old Houses.* Alfred Knopf. 1972.

Thomas, Robert B. *The Old Farmer's Almanac.* 1989.

Turn—of—the—Century Doors, Windows and Decorative Millwork. The Mulliner Catalogue of 1893.

Using Records in the National Archives for Genealogical Research. Number 5. 1990.

Vila, Bob. *Guide to Historic Homes of New England.* Quill William Morrow. 1993.

Whitney, Mary. *Pooleys Across America.* 1989.

Wilbur, Keith C. *Homebuilding and Woodworking in Colonial America.* The Globe Pequot Press. 1992.

Williams, Henry & Ottalie. *Old American Houses, 1700—1850.* Bonanza Books. 1989.

Winchester, Alice. *How To Know American Antiques.* Signet Key Books. 1951.

MAGAZINES

Colonial Homes. Volume 11, Number 4. July—August 1985.
Volume 23, Number 6   November 1997

Country Victorian Volume 11, Number 1. Winter 1998

Decorating Winter 1996—97

Early American Homes. October 1997.

Historic Preservation. National Trust for Historic Preservation. Volume 30, Number 4. October—December 1978.

Old House Journal. Volume XXVI, Number 2. March/April 1998
Volume XXVI, Number 5. October 1998

This Old House. September/October 1997
July/August 1997
January/February 1997

INDEX